GOING NORTH

Memorabilia of Tourism in Alaska, Yukon, and Northern British Columbia

EARLY 1900s TO THE PRESENT

BY STAN COHEN

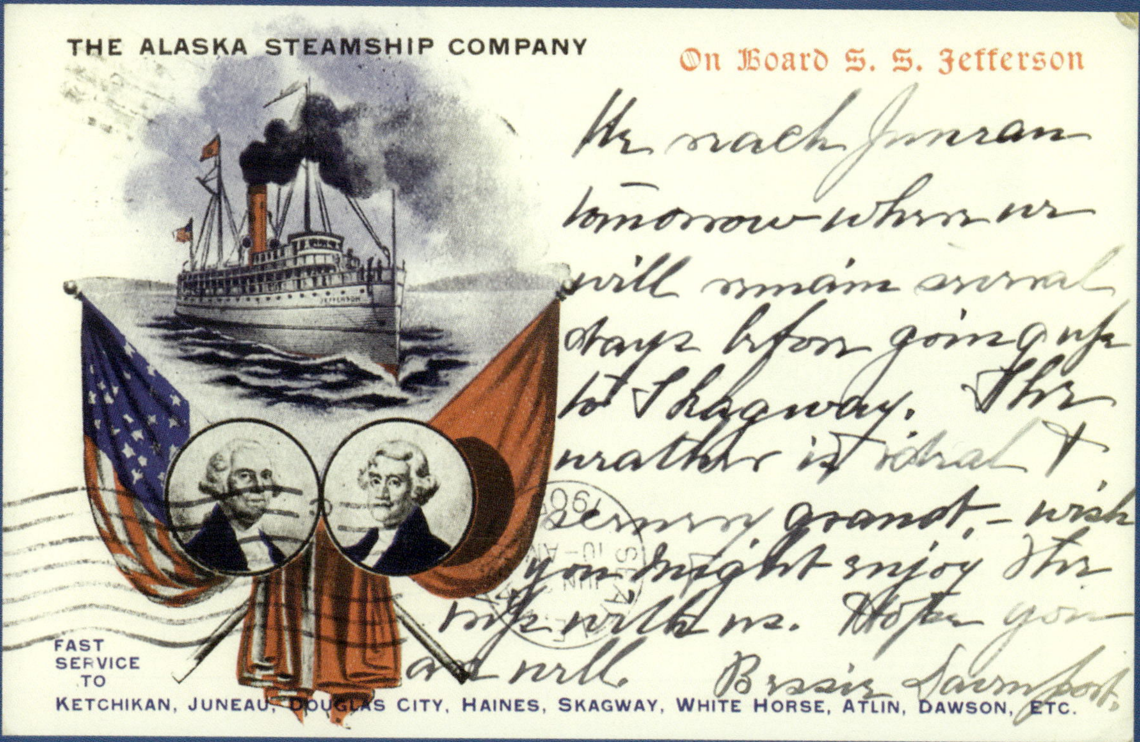

First Printing, April 2024

All the photos are acknowledged to their source when known.
AC is from the author's collection.

LCCN Number: 2023952200

ISBN Number: 978-0-87842-716-1

Printed in India

ALASKA TREASURE SHOP
424 4th Ave. Box 1019
Where you find the Territory's finest and most complete collection of Indian and Eskimo arts and crafts, including:
Ivory Carvings — Totem Poles
Baskets — Moccasins — Mukluks
Parkas — Dolls
Jade and Nugget Jewelry
Paintings by Alaska's Foremost Artists
Write for free catalog

This book is dedicated to my good friends, Ken and Arlene Brovald. They came to Anchorage for Ken's job with the Alyeska pipeline construction project and stayed afterwards. Ken was a railroad "nut" and I published two books for him, stayed at their house when I was in Anchorage researching and selling books, and after they bought The Alaska Treasure Gift Shop, helped them in the store for days at a time. When Ken's health started to fail, they sold the store and after his death, Arlene moved to Washington state.

MP Mountain Press
PUBLISHING COMPANY
P.O. Box 2399 • Missoula, MT 59806 • 406-728-1900
800-234-5308 • info@mtnpress.com
www.mountain-press.com

TABLE OF CONTENTS

ACKNOWLEDGMENTS

Many thanks to the numerous museums, archives, and individuals in the United States and Canada for helping me accumulate the pictorial contents of this book that spans about 50 years. A lot of these photos and maps have been used in my other books on Alaska and Yukon. In addition, I want to thank the following for help: the staff of Mountain Press Publishing Company, especially Jeannie Painter, who did her usual great job on design; Jeff Stevens and Andrea Halland of Missoula, who did the editing and proofreading; Amy Andrews of Missoula, who was my IT person; my friend Michael Gates of Whitehorse, Yukon, who supplied photos; Mickie Lucchetti of Corrington's, Moria Finn of Alaska X; Nicholas McGraw of the Discovery boats; Kasey Gillam of Explore Fairbanks.com; Lauren Taylor of the White Pass & Yukon Route; Bob Schutsky of Bird Treks Tours; Heather of The Santa Claus House; Mark Pavao, who supplied the Pan-American poster; Kathy Burden of Parks Canada: and Dawn Millen of the Alaska Marine Highway System.

The author in front of the old miner's cabin on Arne Erickson's gold claim where he worked in 1963.

STAN COHEN established Pictorial Histories Publishing Co. Inc in 1976 in Missoula, Montana and has authored or co-authored 74 pictorial books and published 150. He has worked in Alaska as a geologist and spent 50 years travelling the North Country from Nome, Attu and Kiska in the Aleutian Islands, all of Southern Alaska, Eagle, Atlin and the major cities of Whitehorse, Dawson City and even Old Crow in the Yukon researching and promoting his North Country books. He lives in Missoula with his wife Anne.

ESCORTED
CRUISE TOURS
ALASKA
YUKON
by
AIR & SEA - 1959
THE 49th STATE
Scenery
Unlimited To

welcome to
ALASKA

INTRODUCTION

This volume is a compilation of 50 years of writing about and collecting items of the varied histories of Alaska, the Yukon, and Northern British Columbia. Much of this has to do with the very large tourist business in the areas. The chapters reflect the history of the steamship companies, the airlines, the railroads, and the various means for vehicle movement between Canada and the mainland of the United States plus histories of tourist towns and sites up to the present day.

The years between the world wars saw a dramatic rise in tourism during the twentieth century, a sharp decline during the Depression years and a vigorous recovery leading up to World War II. Today tourism in the area is an international business with many facets from fishing, hunting, boating, cruises, sightseeing by air and land, hiking, and camping, to some exotic endeavors such as backcountry skiing, and ice climbing. There are many world-famous natural and historic sites to visit.

Alaska has huge areas of not only national parks, monuments, wildlife refuges, and native lands but many thousands of miles of remote accessibility. The Yukon has a very rich history of gold and other mineral mining activity. Of course, the mighty Yukon River dissects both the Yukon and Alaska. Northern British Columbia comes into play with both the Alaska Highway and the routes to the early goldfields, as well as the narrow-gauge railroad entering its borders.

Between the covers, the reader will find a vast display of photos, brochures, postcards, menus, transportation schedules, and other means to lure the tourist north. The postcards range from the very colorful German printed cards of the early 1900s to the much more prolific, so-called linen cards of the '30s, and '40s. They give a good visual account of what the sites looked at the time. So, sit back and enjoy a nostalgic trip starting over one hundred twenty years ago with the end of the Klondike Gold Rush in the Yukon.

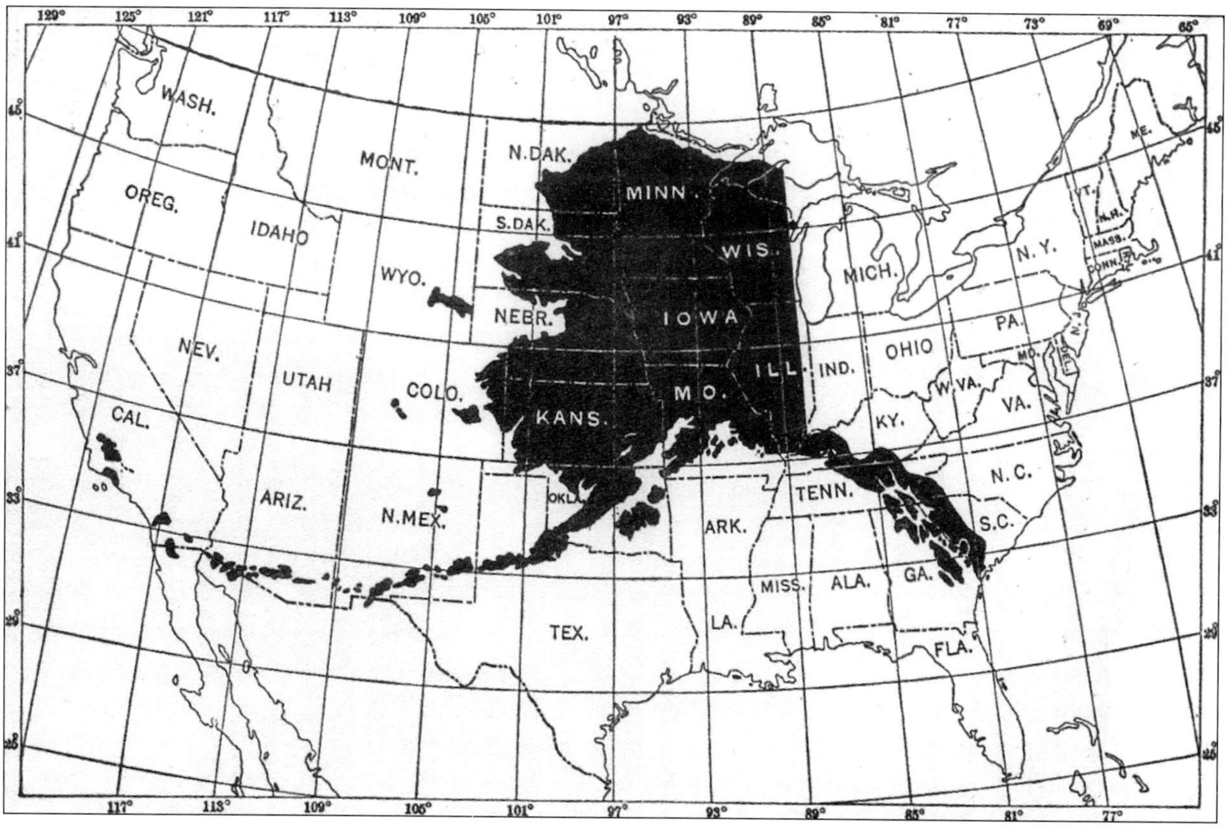

From the 800-piece PAA poster colletion of Mark Pavao of Philadelphia, PA, circa 1935.

A HISTORY OF TOURISM IN ALASKA, YUKON, AND NORTHERN BRITISH COLUMBIA

Tourism in the North Country can be traced back to 1880 with a cruise by The Pacific Steamship Company to Glacier Bay near Juneau, Alaska. With the discovery of rich placer gold deposits in the Klondike region of the Yukon in 1896, this sparked one of the largest "gold rushes" (stampedes) in North American history. By the thousands, both men and women, rushed north to an unknown territory with unimagined hardships on the way. The rush lasted for a few years and then settled down with hundreds of claims staked throughout the Klondike and the establishment of the main town in the area, Dawson City on the banks of the Yukon River.

The bulk of the people headed north were either prospectors or those hoping to make a fortune off the men who worked the claims. Many got rich almost overnight, mainly the ones who were already in the area searching for a big strike, and Dawson City became the largest city in the north with a population of over 20,000 at one time. Many, many books have been written about this part of northern history. The actual rush was over in about two years and soon the life of individual miners phased out and consolidation of claims started. Large corporations moved in with gold dredges and hydraulic mining, decreasing the need for thousands of miners. Dawson City settled down in the early 1900s with most of the amenities of a regular town, but was very isolated from its neighbors to the south. By 1900 the White Pass & Yukon Route had conquered the White Pass out of Skagway, and one could take the train to Whitehorse, Yukon, and then river steamer, 400 miles down the Yukon River to Dawson City. Some tourists ventured to the North, the hard way in the early days, but the opening of the narrow-gauge railroad facilitated the ease of travel for them and also normal traffic for miners, businessmen and others to and from the isolated north country.

Alaska was discovered in 1741 by Russian explorers led by Vitus Bering. He probed part of the vast coast, and Russian traders colonized Kodiak and Wrangell, and founded Sitka as their capital. The US Government purchased the territory in 1867 from Russia for $7.2 million and it became a territory in 1912. But it was a difficult trip for a tourist; and the season was short and there were many inconveniences along the way. Several steamship companies were serving the Inside Passage in the early 1900s and The Alaska Railroad opened a tourist office in Chicago in 1929 offering three coordinated trips: The Yukon Circle, The Golden Belt and The All Rail. All were time-consuming and expensive.

Canadian National Railways operated the *Prince Robert*, one of three coastal passenger liners in competition with the Canadian Pacific Railway's longstanding dominance on the Vancouver–Victoria–Seattle passenger route. The *Robert* could carry 375 passengers and spent part of the 1930s on the tourist runs from British Columbia to Alaska. In September 1939, when World War II started, she and the other two liners were requisitioned for military service as armed merchant cruisers (AMC), as Canada entered the war.

Through the years, interior highways were constructed, including the World War II military ALCAN Highway (Alaska Highway) that opened up a vast area for tourists when the road was opened to civilian traffic. Cruise boats became a comfortable way to explore the region and eventually after the war, airlines began to fly routes to the region from the lower 48. As mentioned, the season was short, usually lasting from the middle of June to late August, and it took time for adequate visitor accommodations to be established.

Today, both Alaska and the Yukon are major tourist destinations for world travelers with vast mountain ranges, glaciers, river travel, water and winter sports. There are historic "ghost towns," but still inhabited and old and present mining activity, fishing, hunting and sightseeing opportunities, and countless other ways to keep a visitor busy. For many people from around the world, a trip to the region is a once in a lifetime experience and a major revenue producer for the region.

In early days, visitors would walk the streets of Sitka and view the many natives selling their crafts. —AC

A Rotary International Convention in Ketchikan, no date.
—Alaska State Library, Skinner Foundation Collection, PCA 44-10-Folder 4

Tourists walking a street in the rain in Wrangell in Southeastern Alaska. —AC

Winter & Pond was one of the earliest photographers during the Klondike Gold Rush and they set up a studio in Juneau to sell photos and souvenirs. Notice the antique camera in front. —AC

In this 1930s view, the Fairbanks Tourist Bureau set up a meeting place to give the tourist information on the area. —AC

Knox Brothers was an early Ketchikan souvenir shop, jeweler, and optician. Note the stand-alone clock in front. A hotel was above the shop. —AC

Tourists gather on Skagway's Moore's Wharf with graffiti prominently displayed on the rocks behind. —AC

Tourists on the dock in the old town of Valdez. The town was destroyed by the 1964 earthquake and had to be reestablished a few miles to the west. —AC

Dear ....:

Well, here I am in Alaska, at last! Right away they started calling me Cheechako (that's Siwash for tenderfoot), and tried to feed me ice worms. Saw the Northern Lights last night, but didn't think they were so hot. The mosquitoes gave me a few points on Alaska, though, and I've met Sam McGee from Tennessee and the Lady that's known as Lou. I've already been in one gold-rush and seen a walrus(h) (tusk! tusk!), ate an Eskimo pie, but haven't seen an Eskimo yet. While out in a poling boat I saw a totem pole and a polar bear. Will send you some nuggets soon as I get some, but all I've found yet is some quart(s)z. Seems like I'm just running around in Arctic Circles, so better close now, with husky greetings from,

....

Native crafts were a big attraction for visitors in Alaska, especially carved ivory tusks. —AC

Bears were and still are a big attraction for tourists, especially in Katmai National Park & Preserve and on Kodiak Island. These are brown bears and one would only want to see one from a safe distance or in a museum. —AC

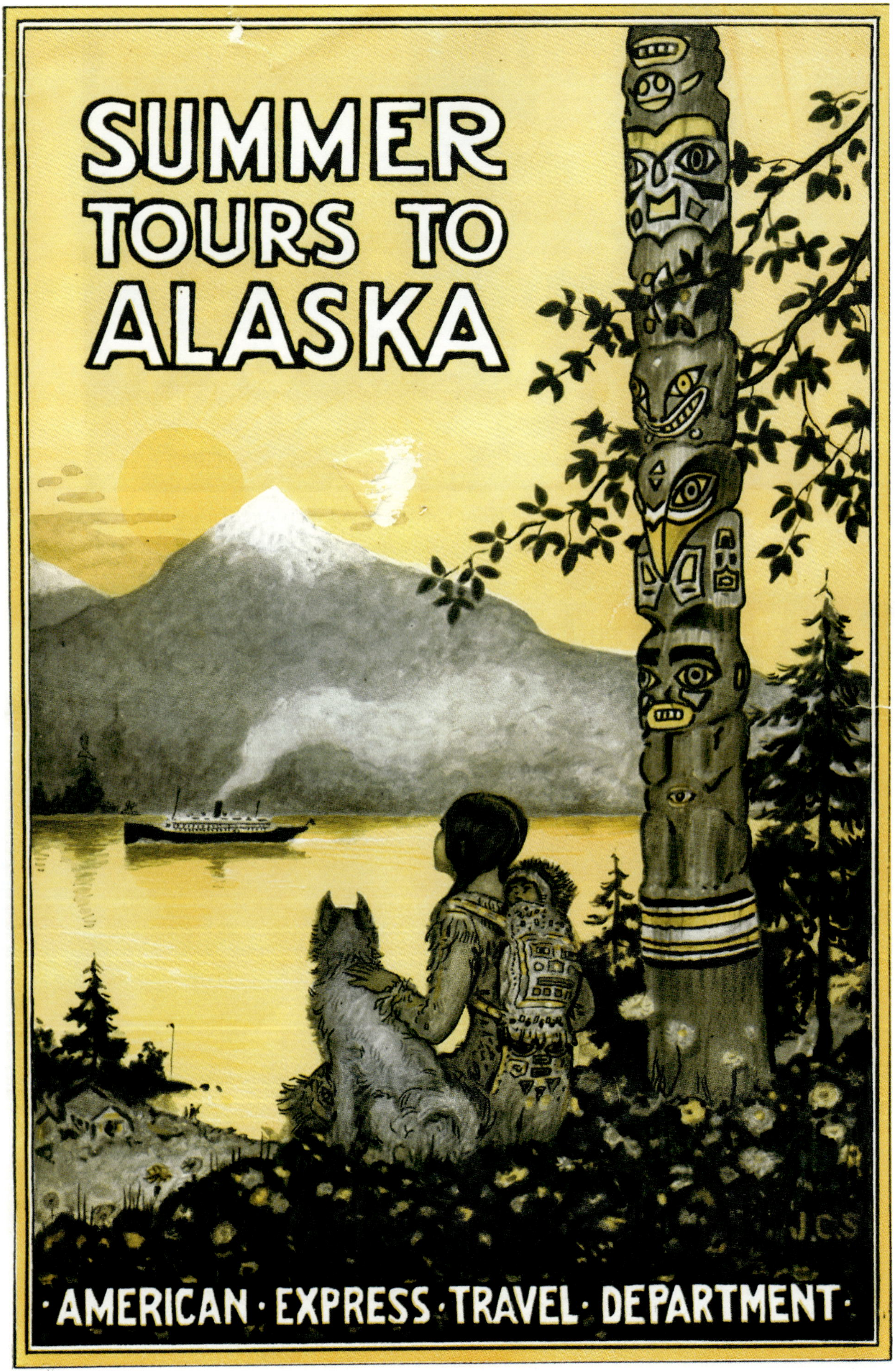
SUMMER
TOURS TO
ALASKA
J.C.S.
·AMERICAN·EXPRESS·TRAVEL·DEPARTMENT·

TOTEM POLES

One who visits southeastern Alaska or the northern British Columbia coast will see a vast array of native-carved totem poles. They are considered sacred but not a religious symbol. They can represent events such as deaths, marriages, and births as well as people and animals. Area tribes such as the Tlingit, Haida and Tsimshian carved totem poles mainly from large red cedar trees found along coastal areas starting well over 100 years ago. The largest displays are in Ketchikan and Sitka, but totem poles can be found throughout the area. Many of the promotional pieces presented in this book included totem poles to entice visitors to come North.

The Nugget Shop on Franklin Street in Juneau was an established souvenir shop for many years. It opened in 1913 and moved to this location in 1924. The largest of the several totem poles in the front was called the Old Witch Totem and was moved from the village of Sukkwan. It was carved in the 1880s and is one of the oldest in Alaska. It underwent restoration and was installed in the State Building in 1977. Note the free-standing clock in front. —US Army Photo

An old postcard view of the Bear Totem Store in Wrangell with many unusual carvings. —AC

A group of tourists at the Totem Bright State Historic Park, 10 miles northwest of Ketchikan. The park was established in the 1930s to preserve the many totem carvings. —Alaska State Library, Skinner Foundation Collection

A 1930s photo of a totem pole in downtown Ketchikan with a steamer docked in the background. —Alaska State Library, Skinner Foundation Collection

Lower left: *A postcard view of the Chief Skowl Arm Totem pole in Ketchikan.* —AC

Lower right: *The Indian Ceremonial House and totem poles at Totem Bright State Historic Park near Ketchikan. This card was printed for Pacific Northern Airlines.* —AC

Top left: *Entrance to Totem Park in Sitka.*

Bottom left: *A group of totem poles in Alaska.* —AC

One of the most famous totem poles of Ketchikan is one of Chief Kian. It is surrounded by the fabled bird Kajuk. Below this bird is an eagle and below the eagle is a wolf. —AC

GLACIERS

Another huge tourist attraction in the past and present are the vast glaciers and ice caps of Alaska and the Yukon. They can be viewed by ship along southeastern Alaska, by road (Mendenhall), hiking to the Portage Glacier from the visitor's center or by air from many airports. One beautiful trip is by boat or plane to view the vast area of Glacier Bay National Park & Preserve out of Juneau. Another can be made by air or hiking in the Wrangell-St. Elias National Park & Preserve in Alaska. Boat tours can be taken to the face of the massive Columbia Glacier out of Valdez, Alaska. There are approximately 664 named glaciers in Alaska. The Yukon has The Kaskawulsh Glacier, which is just one of the numerous glaciers that come out of the St. Elias Mountains within Kluane National Park and Reserve.

A face view of the Mendenhall Glacier with visitors viewing it. There is a US Forest Service Visitor's Center at the site. The glacier is 13.6 miles long and the only large glacier assessable by road, 12 miles from Juneau. There are tours that can be taken to walk on the top.

The large Taku Glacier can be viewed by boat along the Inside Passage. Here, an early steamer is sailing through the calving process ice chunks. —AC

The massive Columbia Glacier near Valdez. An ice chunk on the face has just fallen in the water. Glaciers are constantly moving, but are shrinking worldwide due to climate change. —AC

STEAMSHIPS IN ALASKA AND YUKON

In 1894, six men formed the Alaska Steamship Company which would become the predominant maritime shipping company for passengers and freight to Alaska. Charles Peabody, one of the six, served as president of the company until 1912. The first vessel they purchased was the 140-foot steamer *Willapa*. At the time of the Klondike Gold Rush in the Yukon in 1898, the company began shipping mining equipment and other goods to sustain the gold rush and provide passenger service to Skagway, the end of navigation in Alaska's Inside Passage. The company was bought by the Alaska Syndicate in 1907 to service its copper mining operations in the Wrangell Mountains. It merged with the Northwest Steamship Company, which owned 12 canneries and a retail store and expanded its fleet to 18 ships, retaining the original Alaska Steamship Company name. Service was expanded to serve all of the ports in Alaska and had a virtual monopoly on the Alaskan shipping and passenger service industry.

In 1900, the White Pass & Yukon Route was completed from Skagway to Whitehorse, which enabled much easier access to the gold fields. More fortune-seekers and even tourists headed north by ship. Service was extended to the Valdez-Cordova region and to Nome and the gold mining activity in that area.

In the 1930s the company bought its long-time rival, the Pacific Steamship Company and with the Intercoastal Shipping Act of 1933,

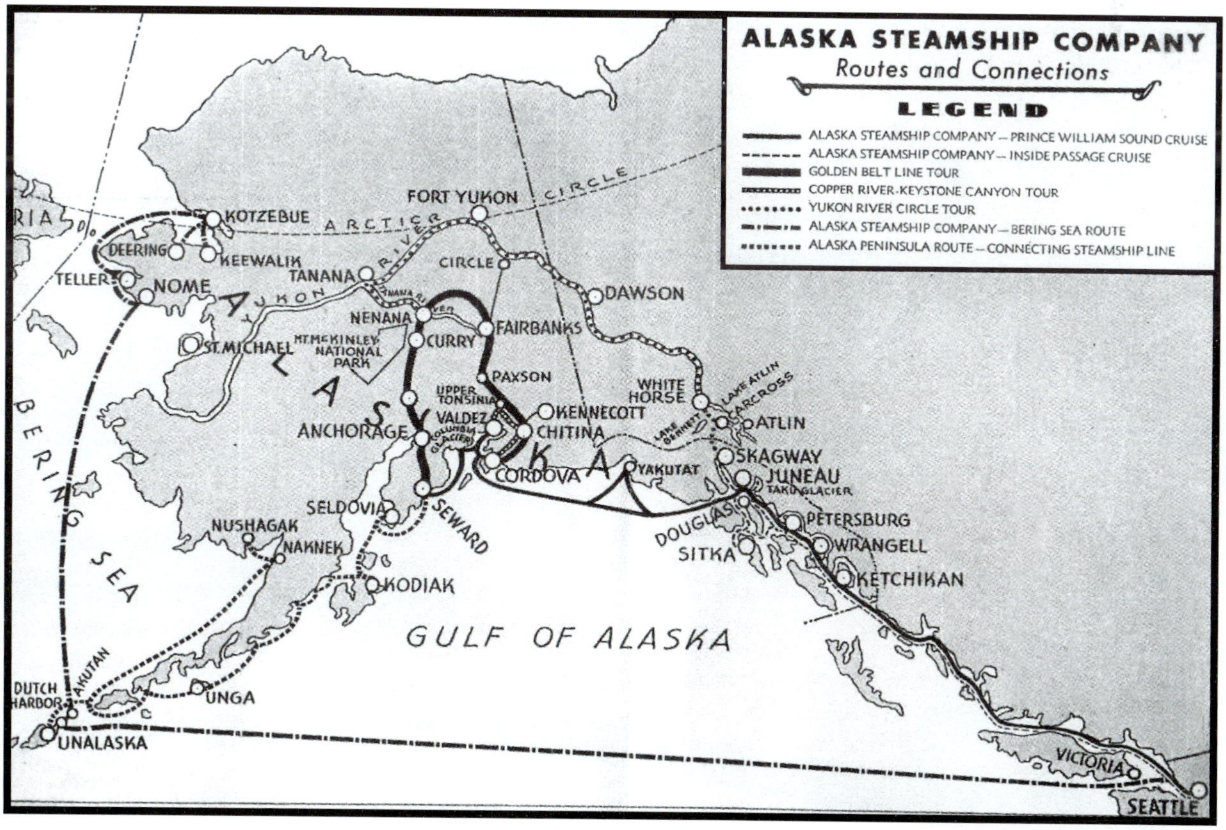

specific schedules and published cargo rates were required. The Federal Government took control of most US registered ships when it entered World War II including the company's 15 ships. Of the 42 ships that served the Alaska trade before the war, only seven were still in service. In 1944 the company was purchased by the Skinner and Eddy Corporation, which also purchased the Northland Transportation Company, the only other major Alaska shipping company to survive the war.

After the war, new competition was established by the opening of the Alaska (ALCAN) Highway and the expansion of freight-hauling airlines. The company added barges, tugs, and container ships to stay in competition as the freight business slowed down. The White Pass & Yukon Route was the first to pioneer containerization. Tourism became the main focus, and in 1946 the company brought their first passenger ship on line, the *S.S. Alaska*. More ships joined the fleet, the *S.S. Aleutian*, the *S.S. Yukon*, the *S.S. Denali*, the *S.S. Mount McKinley*, the *S.S. Columbia* and the the *S.S. Baranof*. The ships sailed the Inside Passage, as well as to Seward, Sitka, Valdez, Kodiak, Seldovia and Cordova. Over 200 passengers could be carried on each trip. The company discontinued passenger service in 1954, in part due to cheaper and faster air service. Its container shipping business continued until 1971, when the entire company went out of business. Between 1898 and 1940 much of the fleet was wrecked and several vessels sank. The rest, were sold, scrapped, or repurposed through the years.

Other steamships companies would follow, including several owned by railroads, but the Alaska Steamship Company was the most dominant. Today, international cruise ship companies have brought passenger service back to Alaska and up to the Yukon with their huge, thousand plus, passenger capacities.

Helen B. McGregor

Greetings from the ALASKA STEAMSHIP COMPANY

Here is a list of your fellow travelers! It is printed as a souvenir and memento of your voyage.

We are happy to have you aboard this ship and our earnest hope is that your trip will be so pleasant you will choose to travel with us again and again!

It is our wish that nothing has been left undone that would have added to your comfort and enjoyment while traveling to and from Alaska—the scenic wonderland of the world!

Alaska is a new land for travel to many people, and as you realize, it is a scenic paradise that must be seen to be fully appreciated. It has countless places and attractions to call you back to see anew or to review.

Tell your friends what indescribable grandeur awaits them in Alaska! And may we now, through you, invite them to come!

We will be grateful for your recommendation of our service, and, please, whenever you "Think Alaska, Think Alaska Steamship Company"!

I want to be alone –
" " " have a good smoke (not me)
To one of the sweetest girls I know
Leah

Aboard Ship!

PERHAPS nowhere in all the world but Alaska can be found such an endless panorama of everchanging vistas, from glass-smooth inland seas to mountain giants bedecked in velvet greens and crystal crowns.

Engulfed in the magic of such setting, life aboard ship is doubly enhanced. Here are hours to relax. To meditate. To take active part in deck games. To stroll in rhythmic step 'round and 'round the decks. To linger and chat with a friend. To know interesting new friendships. To eat delectable foods. To dance. To read a hoped-for book. To have refreshing sleep. To be renewed, to find new life and hope! This ship offers you joy!

Purser will gladly furnish extra copies of this Passenger List for mailing to your friends.

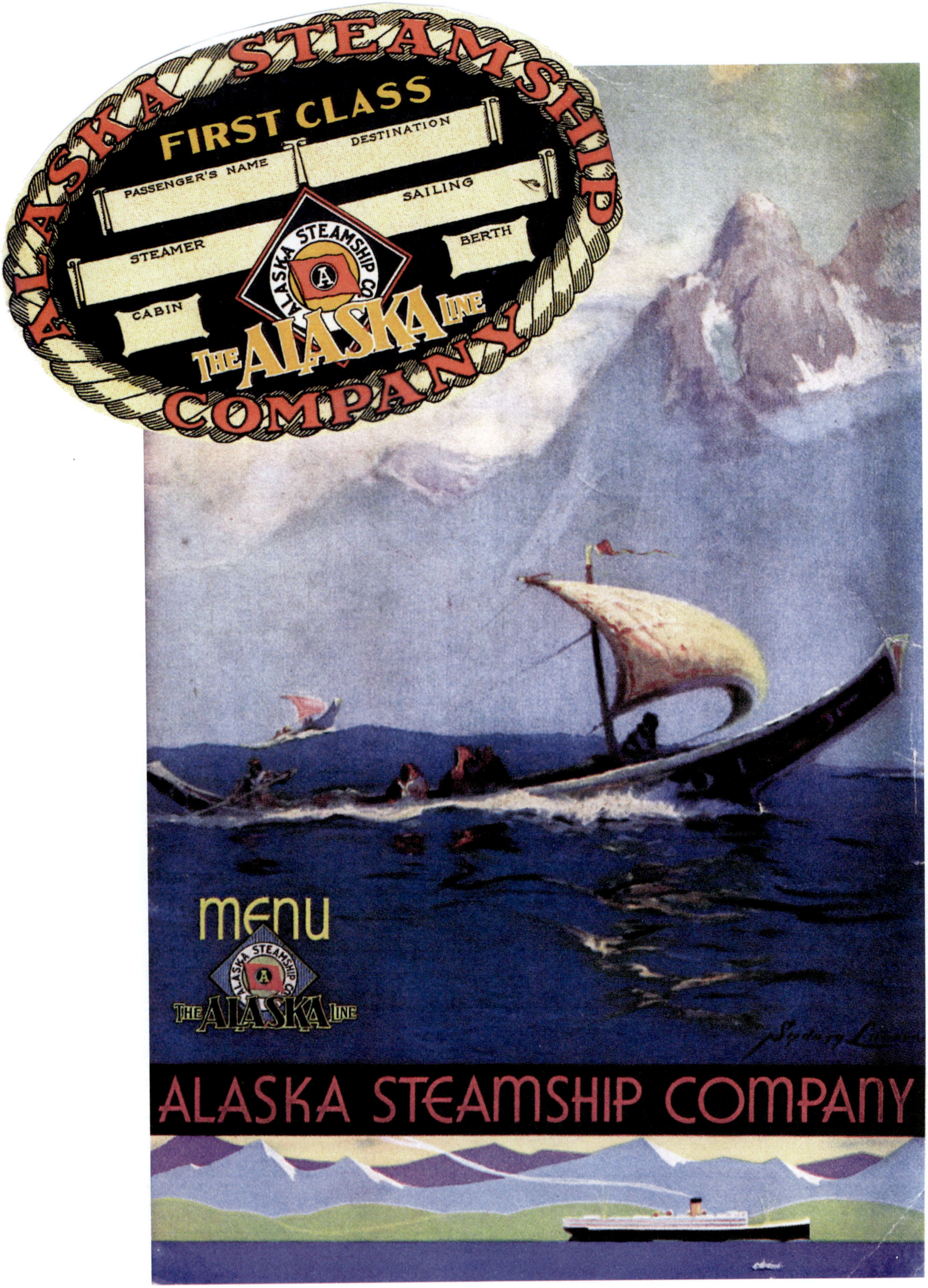
ALASKA STEAMSHIP COMPANY
FIRST CLASS
PASSENGER'S NAME
DESTINATION
STEAMER
SAILING
CABIN
BERTH
ALASKA STEAMSHIP CO
A
THE ALASKA LINE
menu
ALASKA STEAMSHIP CO
A
THE ALASKA LINE
ALASKA STEAMSHIP COMPANY

Autographs

Lucille E. Doty - Bremerton
Bonnie L. Lambert - Bremerton
Dr. McLean Stewards "Aleutian"
Katherine Morrison - San Diego, Calif.
Roy L. Morrison " " " "
Helen M. Geiger - Modesty Circle.
Michael H. Geiger
Louise Sample
Sam Sample
Lew Werner S.F. Cal.

Alaska SERVICES of the ALASKA STEAMSHIP COMPANY

The ALASKA LINE is the only line maintaining service to all parts of Alaska.

On the Southwestern Alaska Route steamers sail from Seattle every Saturday morning at nine o'clock throughout the year, to Ketchikan, Wrangell, Juneau, Cordova, Valdez, Latouche and Seward, with occasional calls at Yakutat. During the winter months steamers on this route also call at Petersburg, Sitka, Haines and Skagway.

The *SS."Yukon,"* on summer announced schedule, connects at Cordova with one of our smaller vessels for Seldovia and Cook Inlet ports. The *SS."Aleutian,"* on summer announced schedule, connects at Cordova with one of our smaller vessels for Kodiak and Kodiak Island ports of call.

On the Southeastern Alaska Route regular service is maintained throughout spring, summer and fall, with sailings from Seattle every Tuesday morning at nine o'clock from early April to early September as shown in announced schedule. Ports of call: Ketchikan, Wrangell, Petersburg, Juneau, Haines (Chilkoot Barracks), Skagway and Sitka. During the winter months service to these ports is offered, as business justifies, by the steamers on the Southwestern route.

To Cannery and Saltery Ports in Southeastern Alaska there is a sailing from Seattle approximately every week—April to September, inclusive. Steamer calls as far north as Juneau, including west coast of Prince of Wales Island and Chatham Strait points.

On the Bering Sea Route we maintain steamer service from Seattle to Nome and/or St. Michael and other ports on Norton Sound during the summer season, when navigation is possible (from about the first of June until the latter part of October). There are two sailings each year, usually about June 1st and August 12th, direct from Seattle to Bering Sea and to Kotzebue Sound points north of Nome.

Steamers operating on all routes endeavor to make connections at all ports with lines operating to the interior.

THE ALASKA LINE — ALASKA STEAMSHIP CO.

Consult your nearest travel bureau or ticket agent, or write us direct, for current sailings.

L. W. BAKER, *Traffic Manager*
Pier Two, Seattle

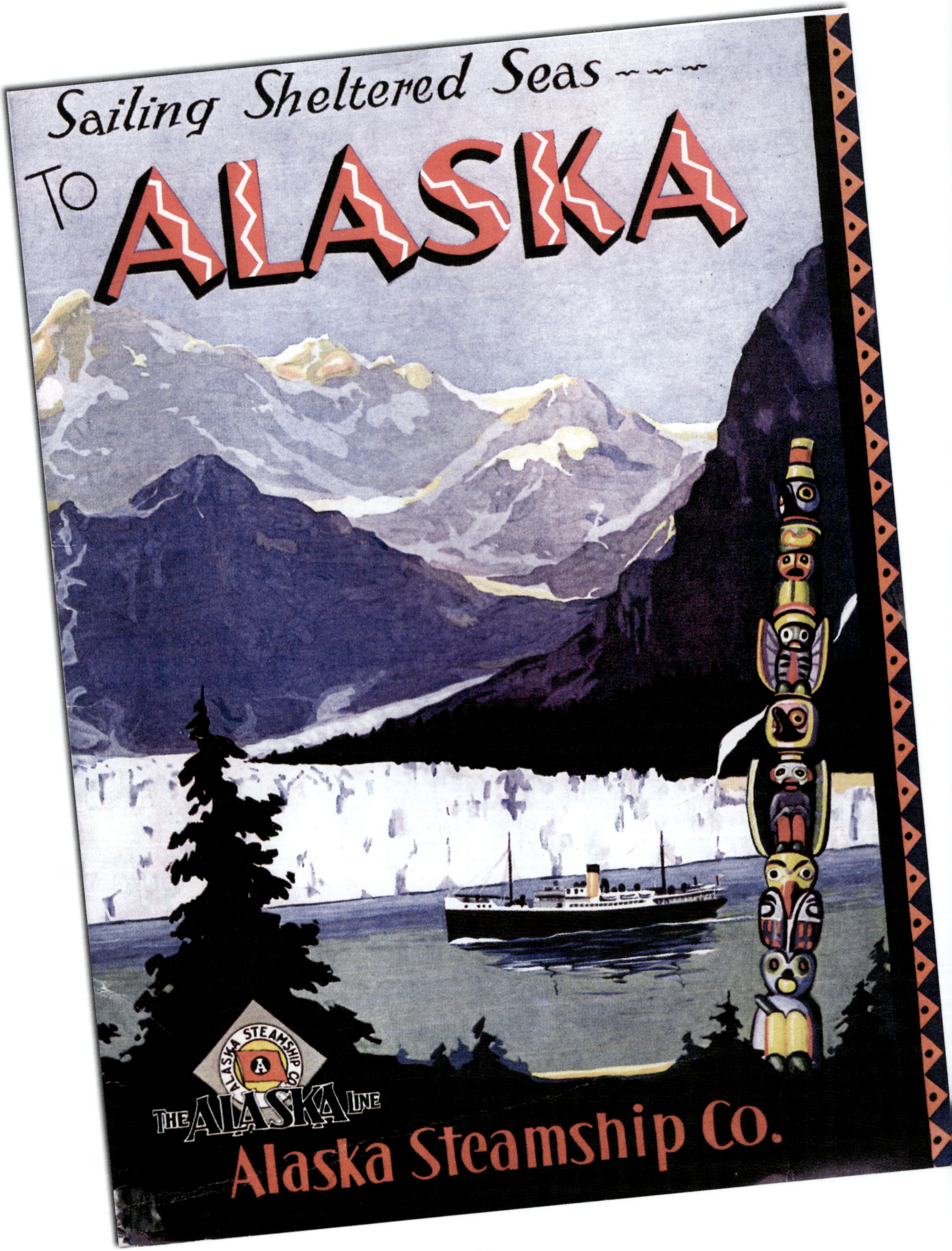
Sailing Sheltered Seas
TO ALASKA
ALASKA STEAMSHIP CO.
A
THE ALASKA LINE
Alaska Steamship Co.

THE ALASKA LINE Fleet

SS. "ALEUTIAN" *(Twin Screw)*

Length, 416 feet
Breadth, 50 feet
Displacement, 9,200 tons
Gross, 6,362 tons

Oscar Nelson
Dorothy Rowe
Florice Merz

SS. "ALASKA" *(Twin Screw)*

Length, 366 feet
Breadth, 49 feet
Displacement, 7,450 tons
Gross, 4,658 tons

Virginia Vanderhoof
Carl H. Hoffman
Ruby I. Hoffman

SS. "YUKON" *(Twin Screw)*

Length, 375 feet
Breadth, 50 feet
Displacement, 8,250 tons
Gross, 5,863 tons

Frank A. Tool
Cleora Tool.

SS. "BARANOF"
SS. "MOUNT McKINLEY"
(Sister Ships)

Length, 373 feet
Breadth, 51½ feet
Displacement, 8,900 tons
Gross, 5,000 tons

SS. "DENALI" *(Twin Screw)*

Length, 335 feet
Breadth, 51 feet
Displacement, 6,480 tons
Gross, 3,365 tons

SS. "COLUMBIA"

Length, 417 feet
Breadth, 49 feet
Displacement, 9,250 tons
Gross, 5,453 tons

PRINTED IN U.S.A. · FRANK McCAFFREY · SEATTLE

The S.S. Northwestern *was built in Philadelphia in 1883, and originally named the* Arazaba. *It was the flagship of the tourist fleet between New York and Havana. It transported troops during the Spanish-American War and, in 1907 was bought by a Seattle steamship company (eventually The Alaska Steamship Company) and sailed to Alaska ports, with a name change to the* Northwestern. *During the 1930s, the ship was out of commission in Lake Washington but in 1940 it was bought by a contractor and hauled civilian workers and military personal to Dutch Harbor in the Aleutians and used as a barracks for the civilian workers. During the attack on Dutch Harbor on June 4, 1942 the ship was heavily damaged by Japanese bombs, but she continued to supply steam and heat for the construction site. It was eventually towed away and sunk in a lagoon.*

THE ALASKA LINE
SEATTLE, WASH.

S. S. YUKON
Capt. LIVINGSTONE
Commanding

Thursday September 21, 1933

LUNCH

Garden Radishes — Dill Pickles — Young Green Onions

Barley Broth — Beef Bouillon

Baked Alaska Halibut Caper Sauce
Grilled French Lamb Chops au Pettit Pois
Baked Pork Spare Ribs Country Gravy
Spaghetti Italian Style

Minced Potatoes — Boiled Potatoes

Hot Slaw

COLD BUFFET

Roast Prime Rib of Beef with Horseradish

Corned Ox Tongue — Boiled Ham

Roast Veal — Tomato Sardines

Potato Salad Served with Cold Buffet Orders

Sliced Cucumbers Cream Dressing

Cream Puffs

Huckleberry Pie — Chocolate Cake

Raspberry Jell-O Whipped Cream

Preserved Cherries — Fresh Fruit

American Swiss or Red Rock Cheese

Coffee Postum Butter Milk Fresh Milk
Black or Green Tea

Arthur Payne, *Chief Steward*

Envelopes for Mailing may be Obtained from Waiter
Please Refrain from Smoking in the Dining Room

ALASKA
STEAMSHIP COMPANY
Copper River & Northwestern Ry.
ALASKA
STEAMSHIP COMPANY
Copper River & Northwestern Ry.
WHEN YOU THINK ALASKA
THINK ALASKA STEAMSHIP CO.
WHEN YOU THINK ALASKA
THINK ALASKA STEAMSHIP CO.
ALASKA
STEAMSHIP CO.

ALASKA
AFTER
A CRUISE ON
ALASKA STEAMSHIP CO.
A
THE ALASKA LINE
you, too, would say—
"No other trip can begin to compare with our all-American trip to Alaska via the Alaska Steamship Company."
"One of the most picturesque, scenic, restful and edifying vacations in this or any other Country."
"It will be my pleasure to recommend your boats without any reservations."
"Food was excellent and well-served."
"Every traveling comfort was there."
"The most wonderful trip I ever had and the most wonderful scenery I ever saw. (I'm a Californian, too)."
An Alaska tour or cruise to fit your time or purse is described in this folder
ALASKA STEAMSHIP CO.
A
THE ALASKA LINE
SUMMER CRUISES
ALASKA STEAMSHIP COMPANY
SEATTLE

THIS IS
Alaska..
Land of Yesterday..Today..Tomorrow!
AGELESS in spectacular scenic grandeur that has been sculptured with all the finesse and art of natural forces . . . born of yesterday from rich legendary lore of totemism into the history of civilized man through turbulent and costly struggle for furs and gold . . . a vacationland distinctly of today, where nature's phenomenal exploitation of beauty is fresh, virile, clean and unspoiled . . . a world vacationland of tomorrow with reserve resources for ages to come . . . this is Alaska! This is where men seek adventure and romance sailing sheltered seas. Northward – north of the setting sun, go these seekers of the strange and beautiful, and you can almost hear their voices as they cry, "Alaska! Alaska!"

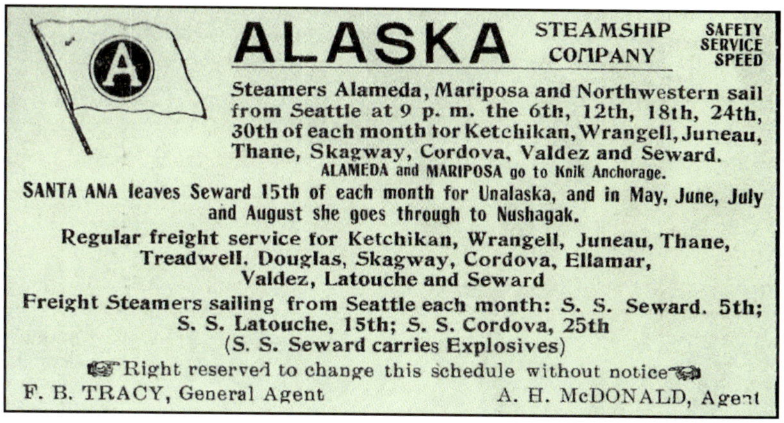
ALASKA STEAMSHIP COMPANY
SAFETY SERVICE SPEED
Steamers Alameda, Mariposa and Northwestern sail from Seattle at 9 p. m. the 6th, 12th, 18th, 24th, 30th of each month for Ketchikan, Wrangell, Juneau, Thane, Skagway, Cordova, Valdez and Seward.
ALAMEDA and MARIPOSA go to Knik Anchorage.
SANTA ANA leaves Seward 15th of each month for Unalaska, and in May, June, July and August she goes through to Nushagak.
Regular freight service for Ketchikan, Wrangell, Juneau, Thane, Treadwell, Douglas, Skagway, Cordova, Ellamar, Valdez, Latouche and Seward
Freight Steamers sailing from Seattle each month: S. S. Seward, 5th; S. S. Latouche, 15th; S. S. Cordova, 25th
(S. S. Seward carries Explosives)
Right reserved to change this schedule without notice
F. B. TRACY, General Agent
A. H. McDONALD, Agent

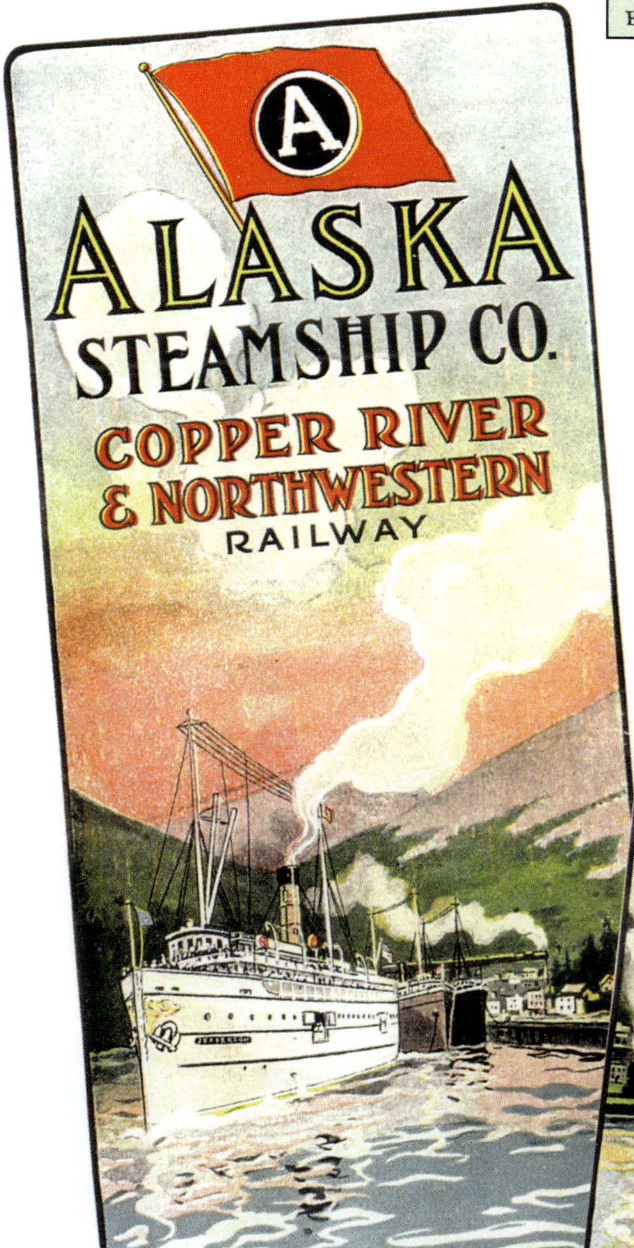
A
ALASKA
STEAMSHIP CO.
COPPER RIVER
& NORTHWESTERN
RAILWAY
R. W. BAXTER
VICE-PRESIDENT
JOHN H BUNCH
GEN'L FREIGHT AND PASSENGER
SEATTLE, WASH.

ALASKA
STEAMSHIP CO.
COPPER RIVER
& NORTHWESTERN
RAILWAY
VICTORIA
A
R. W. BAXTER
VICE-PRESIDENT
JOHN H. BUNCH
GEN'L FREIGHT AND PASSENGER AGENT
SEATTLE, WASH.

ALASKA
AND THE YUKON
1940
ALASKA
AND THE YUKON
1940
CANADIAN PACIFIC
B.C. COAST STEAMSHIPS
Canadian Pacific
CANADIAN PACIFIC
B.C. COAST STEAMSHIPS
Canadian Pacific

ALASKA
ALASKA
IS NEARBY
SEATTLE
SEE YOUR LOCAL TRAVEL AGENT
—or write: H. N. Peterson, General Passenger Agent
Room 157, Pier One, Alaska Steamship Company, Seattle, Wash.
COPYRIGHT, 1941 BY ALASKA STEAMSHIP COMPANY
METROPOLITAN PRESS, SEATTLE
MAY
JUNE
JULY
AUGUST
SEPTEMBER
The Season is Long!
YEAR 'ROUND SERVICE—OF COURSE!
ALASKA
ALASKA STEAMSHIP COMPANY

CRUISING AN AISLE OF ISLES TO

ALASKA

NORTHLAND TRANSPORTATION CO.

S. S. NORTH SEA

MENU

DINNER

A. J. BORKLAND, Commander

Sunday, July 26, 1936

Sardine Canape — Pineapple Cocktail

RELISHES

Sweet Pickles — Pearl Onions — India Relish

Celery en branche — Mixed Olives

SOUPS

Cream of Soubise — Consomme Clear

HOT DISHES

Baked Halibut, Bretonne Sauce, Saratoga Chips

Lamb Tongues a la Vinaigrette

Saute of Veal Kidneys, Madeira Sauce

Raisin Fritters, Lemon Sauce

ROASTS

Roast Young Milk Fed Chicken, Sage and Onion Dressing

Prime Ribs of Beef au jus, Browned Potato

VEGETABLES

Snowflake Potatoes — Boiled Potatoes

New String Beans

Quartered Tomatoes, French Dressing

PASTRY AND DESSERTS

Steamed Fruit Pudding, Spice Sauce

Pineapple Pie — Vanilla Ice Cream — Tutti Fruitti Sundae

Hot Bread — Fruit Cake — Cream Puffs — Assorted Cakes

Assorted Cheese

Dromedary Dates — After Dinner Mints — Salted Assorted Nuts

Nuts and Raisins — Fresh Fruit — Crystallized Ginger — Chocolates

Cafe' Noir

F. L. STEWART, Chief Steward

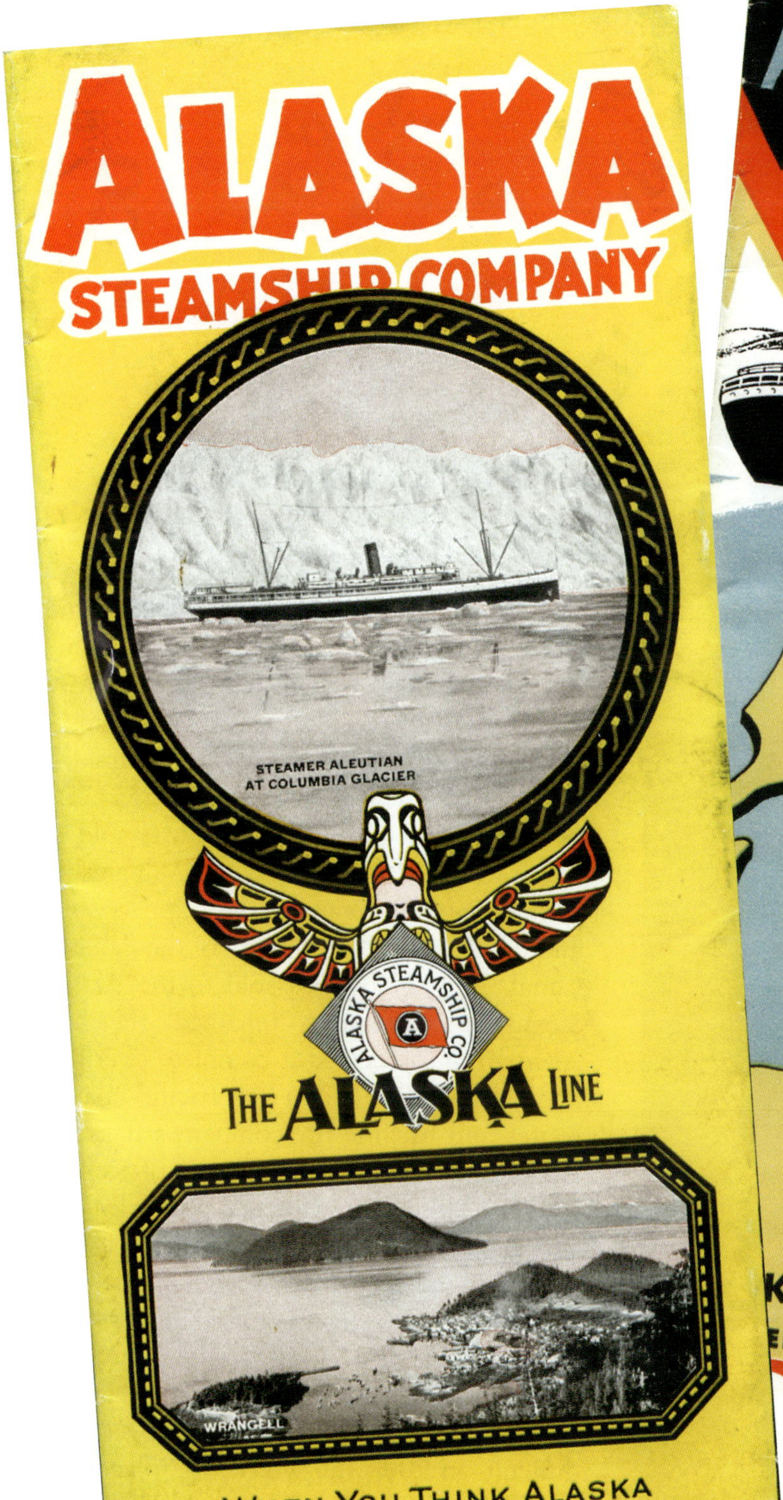
ALASKA
STEAMSHIP COMPANY
STEAMER ALEUTIAN
AT COLUMBIA GLACIER
ALASKA STEAMSHIP CO.
THE ALASKA LINE
WRANGELL
WHEN YOU THINK ALASKA
THINK ALASKA STEAMSHIP CO.

ROUTE MAPS
Southeastern – Southwestern
ALASKA
featuring
FAMED
INSIDE
PASSAGE
ALASKA STEAMSHIP CO.
THE ALASKA LINE
KA STEAMSHIP COMPANY
ER ONE
SEATTLE

The *S.S. Aleutian* had a varied history and a tragic ending. It was built in Philadelphia in 1899 as the *S.S. Havana* for the Ward Line and saw limited service in the Spanish-American War. Then it saw service linking New York with Nassau, Havana and Mexican Gulf ports. The ship was sold in 1905 to the Panama Railroad Steamship Company and renamed the *S.S. Panama* and used during construction of the Panama Canal. In 1927, it was sold to the Alaska Steamship Company, renamed the *S.S. Aleutian* and received a complete overhaul and was transferred to the Pacific coastal routes and became the company's flagship. On May 26, 1929, off the coast of Kodiak Island it struck a submerged pinnacle rock and sank in seven minutes. One crewman died, but the other 153 on board the ship survived. The wreck was found in 2002 and some artifact recovery was initiated, but it had sunk in a deep area, with a strong current and low visibility, which made recovery too difficult. In 2004 the wreck was placed on the National Register of Historic Places.

An Alaska Steamship Company steamer docked, apparently about to leave with well-wishers sending off the passengers. —Alaska State Library, Skinner Foundation Collection

Passengers playing shuffleboard on board a company steamer. Circa 1930s.
—Alaska State Library, Skinner Foundation Collection

Two views on the S.S. Alaska. *The top is the forward salon, the bottom is the dining salon.*
—Alaska Historical Library

PACIFIC COAST STEAMSHIP CO.

Alaska Excursions

SAILINGS—SEASON 1905

EXCURSION STEAMSHIP "SPOKANE"

Between Tacoma and Seattle, Wash., Victoria, B. C., Ketchikan, Metlakahtla, Wrangel, Juneau, Treadwell Gold Mines, Skaguay, Glacier Bay, Killisnoo and Sitka, Alaska.

ALASKA EXCURSIONS. SEASON 1906

The Palatial Alaska Excursion Steamship **SPOKANE**
Will Leave TACOMA, SEATTLE and VICTORIA
JUNE 7, 21. JULY 5, 19. AUG. 2

SECTION OF OBSERVATION ROOM, STEAMSHIP "SPOKANE."

The Steamer "Spokane" will carry only First-class Round-trip Excursion Passengers.

Passengers have the privilege of going on board at Tacoma the evening before sailing.

Passengers via **Great Northern Ry.** take steamer at Seattle. Passengers via **Northern Pacific Ry.** take steamer at either Seattle or Tacoma. Passengers via **Canadian Pacific Ry.** take Canadian Pacific Navigation Co.'s steamer from Vancouver to Victoria, B. C.

This Company's San Francisco and Puget Sound steamers make connections at Seattle with Steamer "Spokane" north and south bound.

EXCURSION RATES

INCLUDING BERTH AND MEALS ON STEAMERS

From **Tacoma, Seattle or Victoria to Sitka and Return**	$100.00
From **San Francisco**—Via Seattle to Sitka and Return by steamer	124.00
From **San Francisco**—Steamer via Seattle to Sitka and return via Tacoma, Northern Pacific Ry. to Portland, Ore., San Francisco & Portland Steamship Company's steamers via Columbia River and ocean to San Francisco, or vice versa	131.35
From **San Francisco**—Steamer via Seattle, returning via Tacoma, Northern Pacific Ry. to Portland, Ore., Southern Pacific Co. (Shasta Route) to San Francisco	136.35
From **Santa Barbara to Sitka and Return** by steamer	139.00
From **Los Angeles to Sitka and Return** by steamer	142.70
From **San Diego to Sitka and Return** by steamer	146.50
From **Eureka to Sitka and Return** by steamer	139.00

3

CANADIAN NATIONAL
ALASKA
AND PACIFIC COAST
CRUISES
VANCOUVER·SITKA·SKAGWAY....11 DAYS
VANCOUVER·SKAGWAY DIRECT..9 DAYS
VANCOUVER·PORTLAND CANAL·STEWART
ANYOX·SOUTH ALASKA.........5 DAYS

Alaska
VIA
TOTEM POLE
ROUTE
C. V. HOWARD,
TICKET AGENT,
101 ADAMS STREET,
CHICAGO.
SUMMER CRUISES
OF THE
PACIFIC COAST
STEAMSHIP COMPANY
LAND OF
MIDNIGHT SUN,
GLACIERS,
THOUSAND
ISLANDS.

Sternwheeling On The Yukon River

The S.S. Tanana *loading wood in 1908. The early sternwheelers were dependent on wood for their boilers and had to make frequent stops along the river to replenish their supplies.* —AC

The S.S. Tanana *at 495 tons was built at St. Michael, Alaska, in 1905. It operated on the side streams of the Yukon River and was sunk in the Thirty Mile River in 1915, but was raised and repaired. The ship sank again in 1921 on the Tanana River, its final resting place. It is shown here at the Northern Commercial Company's dock at Fairbanks on the Chena River.* —Archives, University of Alaska, Fairbanks, Skinner Collection

The S.S. White Horse *at 1,120 tons was built at Whitehorse in 1901 by the British Yukon Navigation Company and rebuilt in 1930. It was beached at Whitehorse and burned to the ground in 1974. She is shown here docked at at a wood coamp for resupply. A good view of the paddlewheel that powered the boat.* —University of Washington, Special Collections, Seattle

After the era of the steamboats closed, many were beached across the Yukon River from Dawson City, perhaps for some to be displayed someday. However, they just sat there for many years decaying. For years anyone really interested in these boats could take the auto ferry across the river and a dirt road passed by the boats. The adventurous ones could walk over to them and climb around them. They have now deteriorated to just wood piles. —AC

Two views of the S.S. Susie *dining room and social hall.* —AC

The S.S. Keno *was built in Whitehorse in 1922 as a side stream freight hauler. It was used to move ore from Mayo Landing on the Stewart River to Stewart Island on the Yukon River. In 1937, it was cut in half and an additional 10 feet was added to its length, increasing its freight capacity. The ship was retired at the close of river navigation in 1951, refurbished in 1960 and sailed downriver to Dawson City, docked on land next to the river and has been worked on periodically. It was designated a national historic site of Canada as it represents sternwheelers used on the Yukon River and its tributaries.* —Michael Gates Photo

MV Klondike Spirit *paddle-wheeler was built in 2007 by two men from Eagle, Alaska, and brought to Dawson City. It is an authentic recreation of early-day paddle-wheelers that plied the Yukon River. Its paddles are attached on both sides instead of in the back. During the season it makes trips up and down the Yukon River passing the native village of Moosehide.* —PR Services/yukonifo.com

The Tarahne *excursion boat at Atlin B.C. was built by the British Yukon Navigation Company (BYN) in 1917 for the Atlin Lake tourist trade in conjunction with the Atlin Inn. In 1928 the boat was cut in half and 41 feet was added in the middle. It could hold 198 passengers. In 1937, due to the lack of business during the Depression, the boat was replaced and in June 1958 was beached at Atlin. Stabilization efforts were initiated through the years and there are now walking tours through the boat in the summer season.* Two other *boats are also on display at Atlin.*—Studio North, WhitehorsePhoto

At 1,040 tons, the S.S. Tutshi *was one of the largest boats on the Yukon. It was built at Carcross in 1918, and its original run was between Carcross and Grahame Inlet on Tagish Lake. It was later converted to an oil burner and carried tourists to the old mining site of Ben-My-Chree off the coast of British Columbia. The owners of the mine eventually imported plants and trees from around the world and converted the area to a beautiful garden spot. The White Pass Company bought the site and operated the boat until 1955. The boat had a crew of 29 and could carry 135 passengers. In 1972 it was beached at Carcross, restored in 1977 by the Yukon government, and later destroyed by an arson fire in 1990.* —AC

The S.S. Tutshi *being loaded at Carcross on Lake Bennett in the Yukon.* —AC

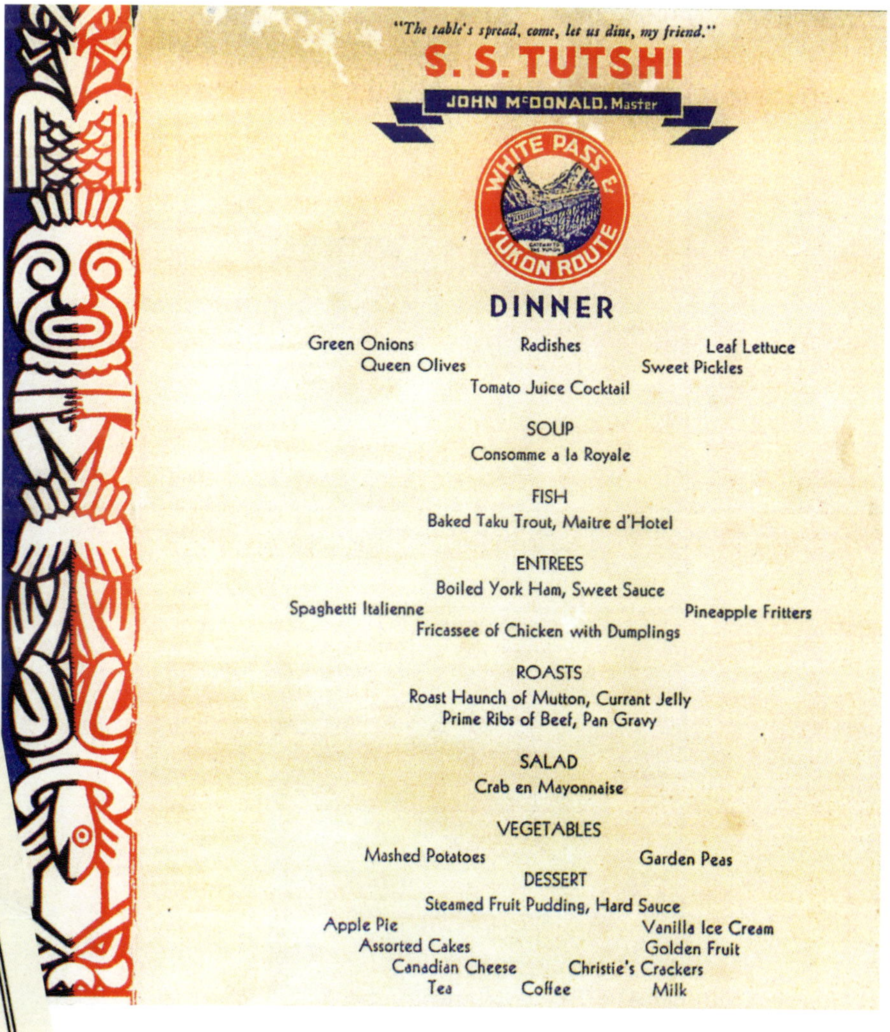

"The table's spread, come, let us dine, my friend."

S. S. TUTSHI

JOHN McDONALD, Master

WHITE PASS & YUKON ROUTE

DINNER

Green Onions — Radishes — Leaf Lettuce
Queen Olives — Sweet Pickles
Tomato Juice Cocktail

SOUP
Consomme a la Royale

FISH
Baked Taku Trout, Maitre d'Hotel

ENTREES
Boiled York Ham, Sweet Sauce
Spaghetti Italienne — Pineapple Fritters
Fricassee of Chicken with Dumplings

ROASTS
Roast Haunch of Mutton, Currant Jelly
Prime Ribs of Beef, Pan Gravy

SALAD
Crab en Mayonnaise

VEGETABLES
Mashed Potatoes — Garden Peas

DESSERT
Steamed Fruit Pudding, Hard Sauce
Apple Pie — Vanilla Ice Cream
Assorted Cakes — Golden Fruit
Canadian Cheese — Christie's Crackers
Tea — Coffee — Milk

River 620

WHITE PASS & YUKON ROUTE
British Yukon Navigation Co. Ltd.

STEAMER TUTSHI

Dining Room Check

TABLE NO. 6

2 SITTING

1ST CLASS

West Bay, Lake Atlin

Atlin Mountains from Atlin Inn

S. S. TUTSHI

JOHN McDONALD
Master

Enroute to Atlin the Beautiful

..............................193........

Llewellyn Glacier, Lake Atlin

MADE IN U.S.A.

THE S.S. KLONDIKE

Two sternwheelers were named the *S.S. Klondike*. They hauled freight along the Yukon River between Whitehorse and Dawson City. The first from 1929 to 1936 and the second from 1937 to the early 1950s. The first *S.S. Klondike* was built in 1929 by the British Yukon Navigation Company, which was a subsidiary of the White Pass & Yukon Route.

In June 1936 *S.S. Klondike* #1 ran aground north of the Thirty Mile section of the Yukon River. Enough of the boat was salvaged to build what is now *S.S. Klondike* #2, which is a National Historic Site, and located for viewing on the bank of the Yukon River at the edge of downtown Whitehorse. When the highway between Whitehorse and Dawson City was opened in the early 1950s, the boat, and other sternwheelers were no longer needed for freight hauling and it was decommissioned. But it had a new life and was converted to a cruise ship plying the Yukon River until finally shutting down in 1955 and was left on the ways at the Whitehorse shipyards.

Parks Canada took the boat as a donation and restoration was started on it until 1966, when the city of Whitehorse agreed to move it to its present location. With further restoration it eventually opened as a major tourist attraction for the city. It has been opened for visitors most years until 2023 when it closed. It is hoped to again open it as it is a fine example of what a sternwheeler looked like in its operating days.

The S.S. Klondike #2 *as it looks on its site today.* —Michael Gates Photo

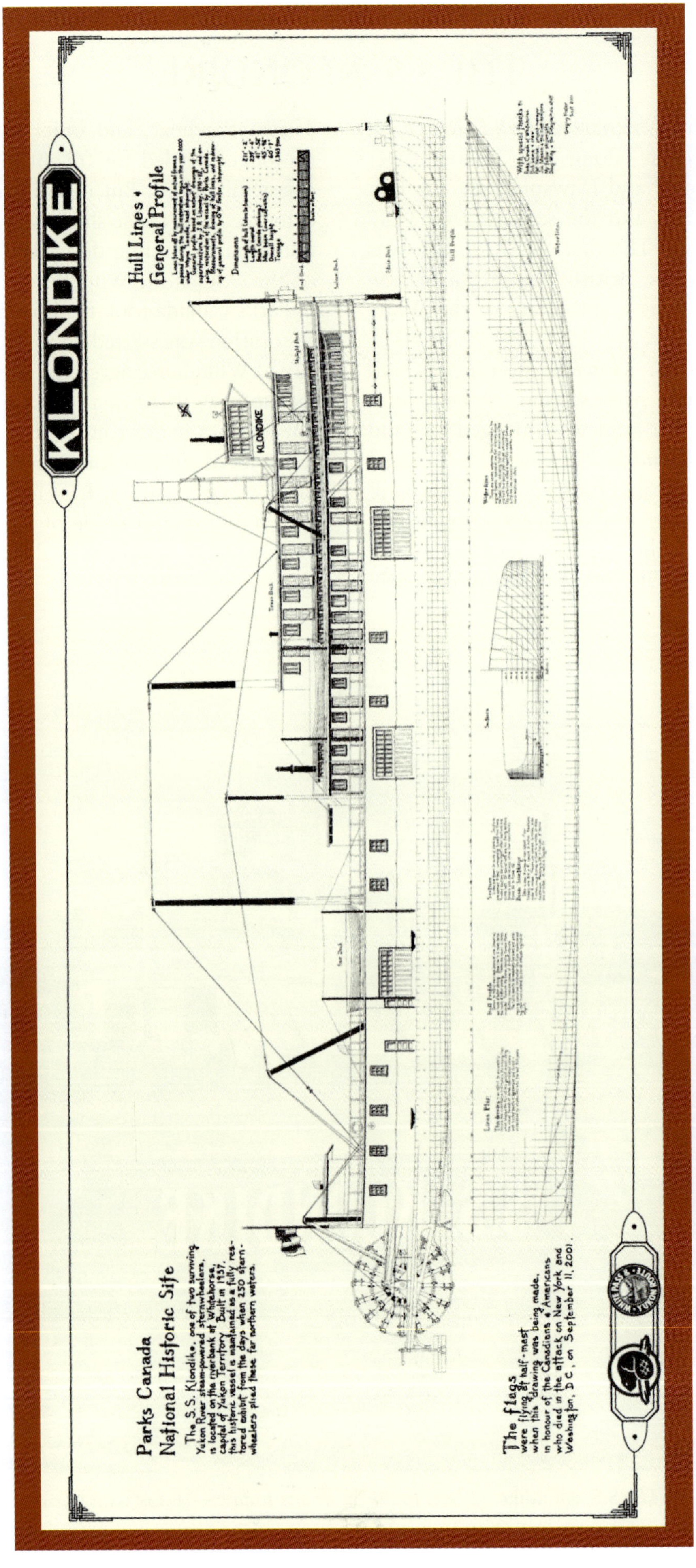

—Parks Canada

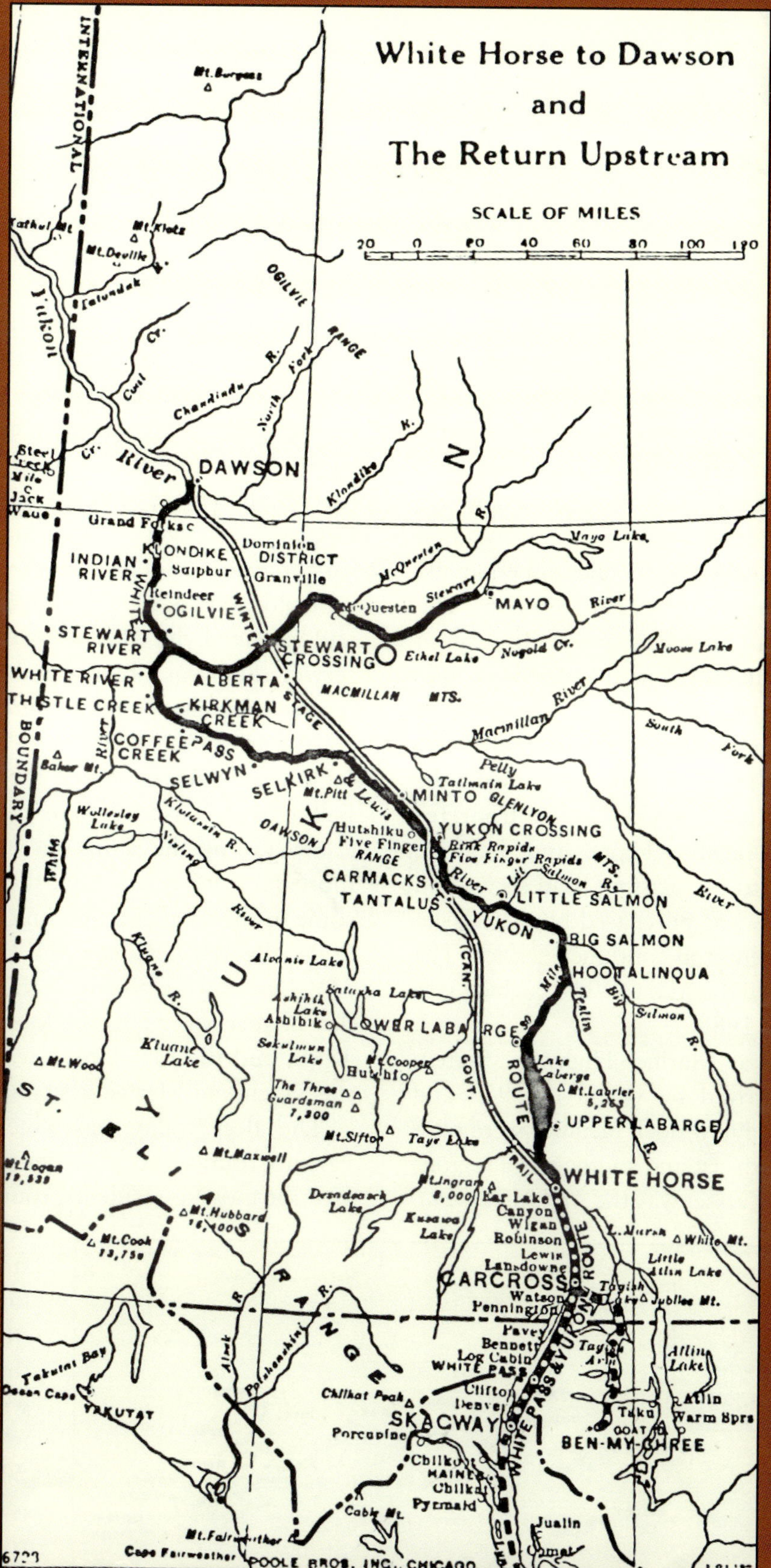
White Horse to Dawson
and
The Return Upstream
SCALE OF MILES
DAWSON
Grand Forks
KLONDIKE
INDIAN RIVER
Sulphur
Dominion
DISTRICT
Granville
Reindeer
OGILVIE
STEWART RIVER
STEWART CROSSING
McQuesten
MAYO
Mayo Lake
Ethel Lake
WHITE RIVER
ALBERTA
THISTLE CREEK
KIRKMAN CREEK
COFFEE CREEK
PASS
SELWYN
SELKIRK
Mt.Pitt
MINTO
Tatlmain Lake
YUKON CROSSING
Five Finger Rapids
CARMACKS
TANTALUS
LITTLE SALMON
BIG SALMON
HOOTALINQUA
LOWER LABARGE
Lake Laberge
Mt.Laurier
UPPER LABARGE
WHITE HORSE
Canyon
Wigan
Robinson
Lewis
Lansdowne
CARCROSS
Watson
Pennington
Pavey
Bennett
Log Cabin
WHITE PASS
Clifton
SKAGWAY
Porcupine
HAINES
Pyramid
Jualin
Atlin Lake
Atlin
Warm Sprs
Taku
BEN-MY-CHREE
Jubilee Mt.
Tagish Lake
WHITE PASS & YUKON ROUTE
INTERNATIONAL BOUNDARY
MACMILLAN MTS.
OGILVIE RANGE
ST. ELIAS RANGE
Mt.Logan
Mt.Wood
Mt.Hubbard
Mt.Cook
Mt.Sifton
Mt.Maxwell
Kluane Lake
Yukon River
Pelly River
Macmillan River
YAKUTAT
Chilkat Peak
Mt.Fairweather
Cape Fairweather
POOLE BROS. INC., CHICAGO

THE ALASKA MARINE HIGHWAY

As one takes a trip up or down Alaska's Inside Passage it is obvious that a boat or plane is the only way to see this majestic area, with its glaciers, flowing into the sea; its vast forests, which have been heavily harvested; and the deep fjords, typical of those in Scandinavia. The Alaska Marine Highway operates along this route but also to the Aleutian Islands, Kodiak, Prince William Sound, and ports of call from Bellingham, Washington, to Prince Rupert, British Columbia.

In all, there are 32 terminals throughout Alaska, British Columbia, and Washington providing service for local residents in the mentioned areas, a freight system and an avenue for tourists. The routes are southeast Alaska, cross-gulf service, southwest Alaska, and the British Columbia coast.

In 1948, two Haines residents started the Chilkoot Motorship Lines using a converted World War II LCT-Mark VI landing craft and named it the *MV Chilkoot*. It offered weekly service from Tee Harbor (north of Juneau) to Haines and Skagway, connecting Juneau to the existing road service. In 1951, the company was purchased by the Alaska territorial government and continued service. The *MV Chilkat* replaced the *MV Chilkoot*, which was decommissioned in 1988.

The new Alaska Marine Highway System (AMHS) was approved by voters in 1959 and four new vessels and new dock facilities were built throughout the southeast and southcentral regions of Alaska. The first vessel was the *MV Malaspina*, followed by the *MV Matanuska* and the *MV Taku*. In 1960 the ocean-certified MV Tustumena was completed. The *MV Chilkat* was moved to Prince William Sound and started service to the southcentral area. In 1969, the *MV E.L. Bartlett* was added until finishing service in 2004.

In 1967, two separate instances stopped ferry service between the AMHS southern terminal at Prince Rupert, British Columbia, and Seattle, Washington. A slide blocked the Alaska Highway going north and a British Columbia ferry ran aground limiting passenger service between Prince Rupert and Seattle. None of the ferries being used had the ocean-going certification required to carry passengers, which made a real hardship for the local residents. To solve the problem, the year-old *MV Stena Britannica* was purchased and renamed the *MV Wickersham* and put into service. She was not really adapted to this new service and the *MV Columbia* replaced her in 1974.The southern terminus of the AMHS was established and remained there until moving to Bellingham, Washington in 1989.

Several of the ships were stretched to give more capacity which took them out of service to some of the smaller communities in the system. In 2004, the *MV LeConte*, *MV Fairweather*, and the *MV Lituya* were added to the system to provide day boat service. The *MV Kennicott* was added in 1998, and the *MV Lituya* was moved to service the Ketchikan-Metlakatla route.

The fleet today has nine vessels operating various routes and provides a very valuable service for moving residents, tourist, and cargo with vehicle storage and staterooms for the longer routes. The *MV Chenega* and the *MV Fairweather* were sold to a Spanish Company in 2021. The highway is the only marine route recognized as a National Byway and All-American Road.

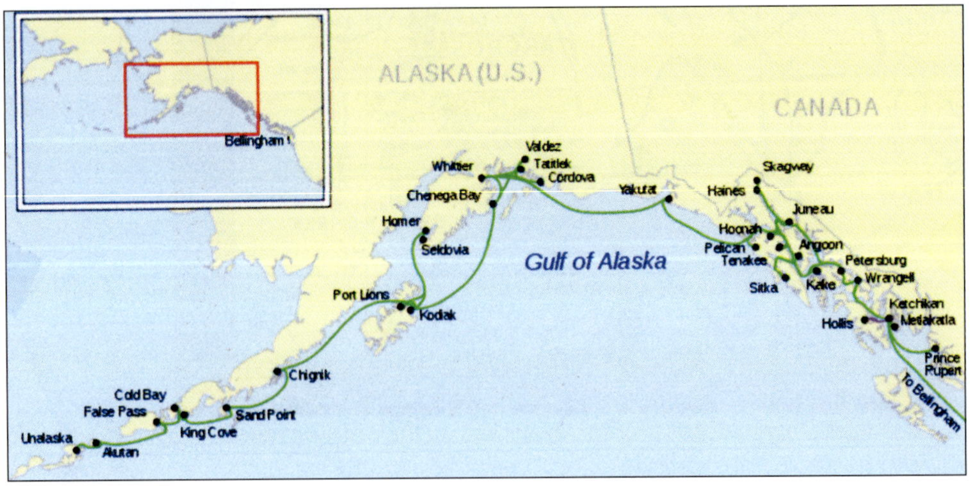

AIRLINES

The following is a brief description of aviation companies that provided service in the North Country, most of them are out of business now. The early, and long gone local flying services continued to merge with one another and a number of name changes were made through the years. There are still mainly local aviation companies that provide service to remote areas and to the many natural and historic sites and lodges, known by the common term, "Bush Pilots."

"Kirk" Kirkpatrick founded Cordova Air Service in 1934 with some local Cordova businessmen. Merle K. "Mudhole" Smith became president after Kirkpatrick's death in 1934. By 1939, the airline had services to Chitina and McCarthy and later to Anchorage, Wrangell, Petersburg and Juneau. Smith later flew for other companies but in 1944 returned to Cordova A/S, which at that time was down to one plane. Smith obtained more planes, and the airline started to rebuild. When the mines at Kennecott closed, which was the airline's biggest customer, the airline developed a popular tourist business to the historic mine. It also started flights to Dawson City, Yukon in 1965. In 1968, the airline merged with Alaska Airlines and the airport at Cordova is now named The Merle K. (Mudhole) Smith Airport.

In 1946, pioneer Alaska aviator Bob Reeve purchased a military DC-3 aircraft and began flying it between Seattle and Anchorage with stops in Juneau, Yakutat, and Annette Island (Ketchikan). Reeve purchased another DC-3 (eventually operating four) and obtained a license to fly between Anchorage and Attu Island in the far Aleutian Chain. In 1947, Reeve Aleutian Airways was incorporated. Pacific Airmotive was doing maintenance for the airline, and in 1950 Reeve bought the business and renamed it Reeve Airmotive. The local airport, Merrill Field, was to be closed in 1952 but it remained open for Reeve and private aircraft. The airline bought different aircraft through the years and expanded to Kodiak with contracts for the government-constructed DEW Line. Reeve moved to the Anchorage International Airport and purchased more modern aircraft, including jets. Its airline's main business was the Aleutian Chain but flew to other parts of the state as well as Seattle-Tacoma and two Russian cities. In 2000 the airline ceased business due to high fuel costs and increased competition.

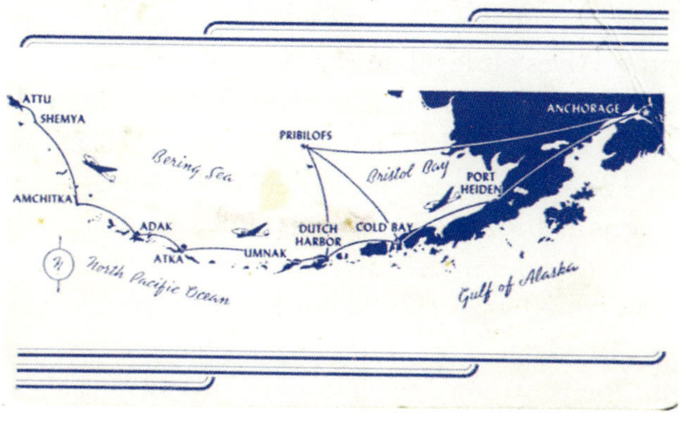

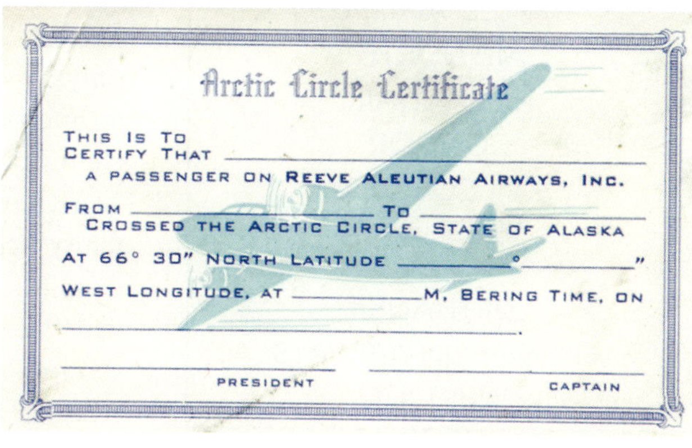

Arctic Circle Certificate

THIS IS TO CERTIFY THAT ______

A PASSENGER ON REEVE ALEUTIAN AIRWAYS, INC.

FROM ______ TO ______

CROSSED THE ARCTIC CIRCLE, STATE OF ALASKA

AT 66° 30" NORTH LATITUDE ______ ° ______ "

WEST LONGITUDE, AT ______ M, BERING TIME, ON ______

______ PRESIDENT ______ CAPTAIN

Noel Wien learned to fly in 1921 and was a well-known barnstormer. He had a charter service out of Fairbanks in 1924, which became the first airline in Alaska. He incorporated Northern Air Transport in 1929 and changed its name to Wien Alaska Airlines in 1936. He expanded in the 1930s, taking over other air services. Its main routes were north of Fairbanks. In 1966 the airline was renamed Wien Air Alaska and two years later merged with Northern Consolidated Airlines to form Wien Consolidated Airlines A change of name back to Wein Air Alaska occurred in 1973 and it continued service until it ceased operations in mid-1984.

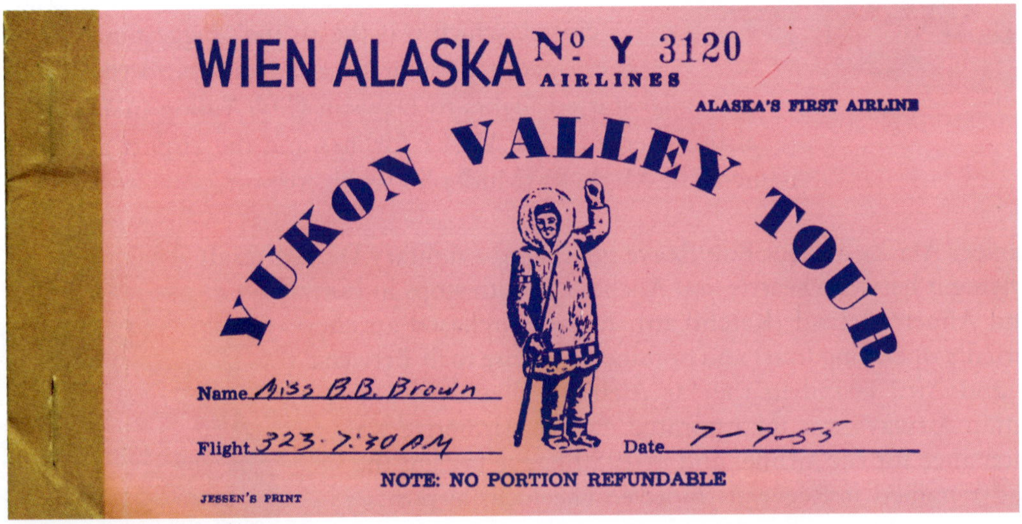

AIRLINES SERVING ALASKA AND THE YUKON

ALASKA AIRLINES
AMERICAN AIRLINES
HAWAIIAN AIRLINES
DELTA AIRLINES
UNITED AIRLINES
AIR NORTH
ICELANDAIR
CONDOR
SUN COUNTRY
(summer only)
AIR CANADA
LUFTHANSA
ALL NIPPON AIRWAYS
WESTJET

MARKAIR began as Interior Airways in 1946, carrying cargo only. When the Alyeska Pipeline started construction, the airline serviced the construction with large cargo aircraft. It changed its name to Alaska International Air in 1974 and to MARKAIR in 1984 and started its passenger business. After many acquisitions it became the largest airline in Alaska. It expanded service to cities in the lower US but went bankrupt in 1992. It restructured itself and established a hub in Denver, serving many American cities but also keeping service in Alaska. The airline was forced to shut down in 1995.

In 1927, Pan American World Airways was founded by Juan Trippe with a merger of three smaller air services. Originally, the airline flew the Miami to Havana route, but Trippe envisioned a worldwide airline in the future, which he achieved by the 1930s, establishing routes all over the world with newly designed flying boats. Pan Am became known as America's Airline. In 1932, it expanded its service to Alaska, purchasing two existing carriers, Pacific International Airways and Alaska Airways, and began service between Anchorage, Fairbanks, and Whitehorse to the lower US with occasional flights to Juneau. Pan Am ceased their Alaska operations in 1978 and declared bankruptcy in 1991, ending a very historic company.

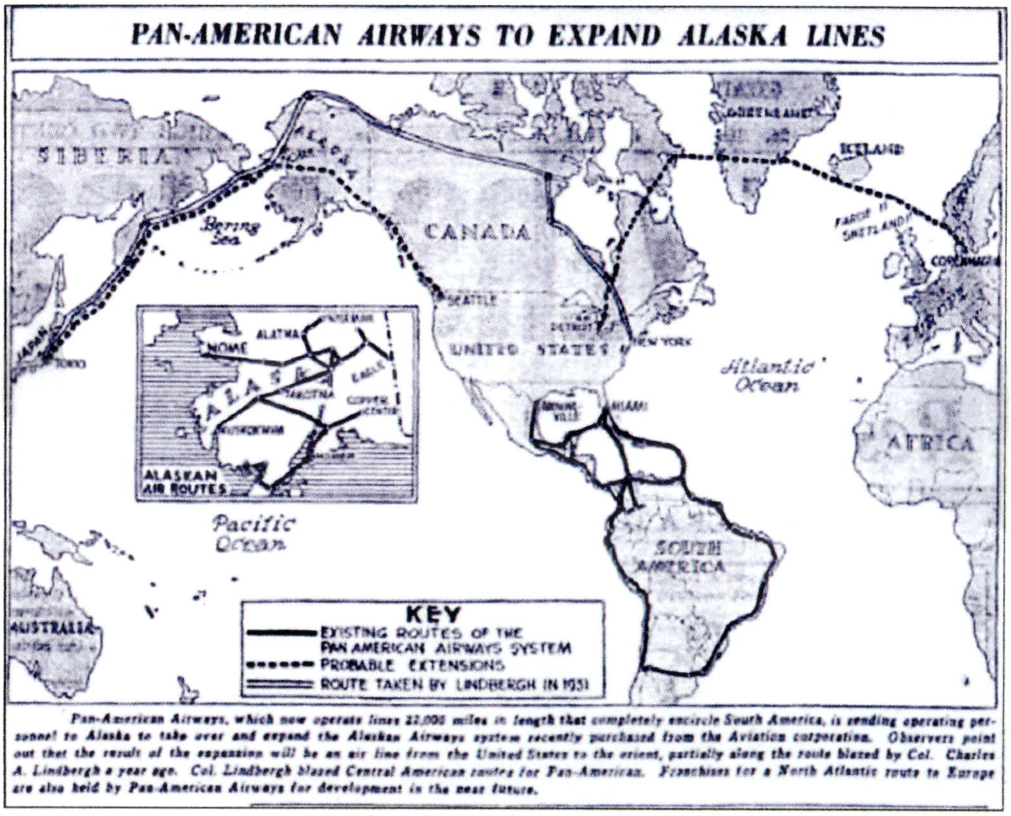
PAN-AMERICAN AIRWAYS TO EXPAND ALASKA LINES

Pan-American Airways, which now operate lines 22,000 miles in length that completely encircle South America, is sending operating personnel to Alaska to take over and expand the Alaskan Airways system recently purchased from the Aviation corporation. Observers point out that the result of the expansion will be an air line from the United States to the orient, partially along the route blazed by Col. Charles A. Lindbergh a year ago. Col. Lindbergh blazed Central American routes for Pan-American. Franchises for a North Atlantic route to Europe are also held by Pan-American Airways for development in the near future.

Map from Chicago Tribune, August 24, 1932

AIR NORTH
Yukon's Airline

Air North operates as Air North Charter and Training Ltd. It is billed as Yukon's Airline. It was founded in 1977 by Joe Sparling and Tom Woods with a single Cessna 206 doing charter operations and freight hauling. They later acquired several DC-3s and a DC-4 and kept adding to their fleet. In the 1990s, more modern turboprop aircraft were acquired and by 2000 jet service was introduced. Its main base is in Whitehorse with secondary bases in Dawson City and Vancouver, British Columbia, and has scheduled cargo and passenger flights all over the Yukon and to Ontario. Its charter business covers the western US and Canada with seasonal fishing and cruise ships excursions.

PenAir

PENINSULA AIRWAYS was founded in 1955 by Orin Seybert and became the second largest commercial airline in Alaska. In 1991, its name was changed to PenAir with headquarters in Anchorage and serviced towns and villages as far out as the Aleutian Islands. It had a code sharing policy with Alaska Airlines and subcontracted with Reeve Aleutian Airways. Eventually, it expanded to the lower US with hubs in Boston, Denver, and Portland, servicing small airports all over the country. The company went bankrupt in 2017 and its assets were bought by Raven Air.

Art Woodley founded Woodley Airways in 1932 with two aircraft. He flew mainly to the Bristol Bay area and secured several mail routes. He renamed his fledging airline, Pacific Northern Airways and to Pacific Northern Airlines in 1945. The airline merged with Western Airlines in 1967.

Alaska Southern Airways operated for only two years, 1932–34, under this name. It was acquired by Pan Am in 1934.

Alaska Coastal Airlines was formed in 1939 through a merger between Alaska Air Transport and Marine Airways, and operated throughout southeastern Alaska. It merged with another airline in the same region, Ellis Air Lines in 1952 and the combined name was Alaska Coastal-Ellis Airlines. It flew World War II surplus aircraft, the Grumman Gooses and the upgraded PBYs. The airline was taken over by Alaska Airlines in 1968.

Northern Consolidated Airlines (NCA) was founded in 1947 in a merger of Northern Airways, Northern Air Service, Walatka Air, and Ray Peterson Flying Service. Peterson was named president of NCA. In 1968, the airline merged with Wien Alaska Airlines and a new name was adopted Wien Consolidated Airlines.

Northwest Airlines was founded in 1926 under the name Northwest Airways with its base in Detroit, Michigan. It flew mail routes, mainly in the midwestern area of the US. Soon it also started carrying passengers and in 1928 started service to Winnipeg, Manitoba, Canada. The next year, the airline was bought out and in 1934 became Northwest Airlines. It started the first direct flights to Japan via Alaska in 1947 and other flights throughout Aisa and underwent another name change to Northwest Orient Airlines but also expanded service to Europe. In 1986, the airline merged with Republic Airlines and its name changed again back to the original, Northwest Airlines. Bankruptcy protection was filed in 2005 and three years later the airline merged with Delta Airlines, which still services Alaska, and the Northwest Airlines brand name was retired.

—Ingrid Barrentina photo, Alaska Airlines

ALASKA/HORIZON AIRLINES

From its founding as McGee Airways in 1932, Alaska Airlines has become the seventh largest airline in North America with its primary hub, of five, and its headquarters at SeaTac Airport in Washington State and serving 115 destinations, along with Horizon Air in the United States, Canada, Mexico, Costa Rica, and Belize in Central America.

Linious "Mac" McGee flew the first service between Anchorage and Bristol Bay with unscheduled flights when there were passengers or cargo. He sold his fledgling airline in 1934 to Star Air Service, which became a dominant airline in Alaska. Star purchased Alaska Interior Airlines in 1937 and Star Air Lines became the official merged name. In 1941 a businessman purchased the airline and bought three other airlines in Alaska and changed the name to Alaska Star Airlines with another name change in 1944 to its present Alaska Airlines.

World War II was a tough time for the airline but it bought its first multi-engine aircraft, the Lockheed Model 18 Lodestar. After the war many surplus aircraft were purchased and it had a large charter business. In 1949, it operated helicopters to support oil exploration on the North Slope and helped carry Jewish refugees from Europe to the new state of Israel. The 1950s saw an expansion of the airline with new aircraft and leadership. The 1960s saw the airline enter the jet age with Boeing and Convair aircraft and Lockheed civilian Hercules model aircraft for hauling drilling rigs to the northern oil fields.

The airline purchased Alaska Coastal Airlines and Cordova Airlines in 1968 and in the 1970s had flights to Siberia in the Soviet Union and to Seattle from Alaska. One of its 727-100 aircraft crashed in Juneau in 1971, killing 111 people. The iconic logo on its aircraft tails was adopted as an image of a smiling Eskimo and is still in use. Tourism brought much more business with flights to and from regional hubs in the US. With new jet aircraft in 1999, the airline started service from Anchorage to Chicago and in the early 2000s from different cities in the continental US and Hawaii. Combination cargo and passenger aircraft were also put into service.

A group of venture capitalists, headed by Milt Kuolt, founded Horizon Air in 1981 to start service between Yakima, Pasco, and Seattle, Washington. In the early 1980s Horizon aquired Air Oregon and Transwestern Airlines, expanding its presence in the West. Alaska Air Group, Inc. acquired the airline in 1986. Horizon operates and maintains its own aircraft, but Alaska Airlines handles all the other aspects of running a regional airline and all its aircraft were rebranded to feature the Alaska Airlines logo.

The Alaska Air Group was formed in 1985 as a holding company for Alaska Airlines and a year later Horizon Air and Jet America Airlines followed. A subsidiary of the Air Group, McGee Air Services, handles ground operations, aircraft cleaning, and wheelchair services for Alaska Airlines. Virgin America was folded into the Air Group in 2016 and merged it into Alaska Airlines in 2018.

GROUND TRANSPORTATION

Alaska, Yukon, and British Columbia comprise vast territories with many obstacles to construct any kind of suitable vehicle accessibility. The Alaska (ALCAN) Highway is a good example of this and a great percentage of the area covered in this book can only be reached by air or on the coastal waters or rivers. After the Alaska Highway opened in 1942 there was a thought to complete it from Fairbanks to Nome, but construction obstacles and cost prohibited this undertaking. There was even some talk about building a railroad to Nome but the same problems were encountered. There are highways servicing the towns and villages on the Kenai Peninsula as well as many other villages and towns in Alaska and Yukon. Several roads leading out of Nome to Teller and Council, allow a viewing of the three locomotives of the Council City & Solomon River Railroad, known as "The Last Train to Nowhere," which were abandoned in 1906.

The Steese Highway runs through the interior of Alaska for 161 miles from Fairbanks to Circle, a town on the Yukon River. It was completed in 1927 and named for US Army General James G. Steese, a former president of the Alaska Road Commission (ARC). The first 81 miles are paved, but around the town of Central the highway turns to dirt and gravel and is narrow and winding.

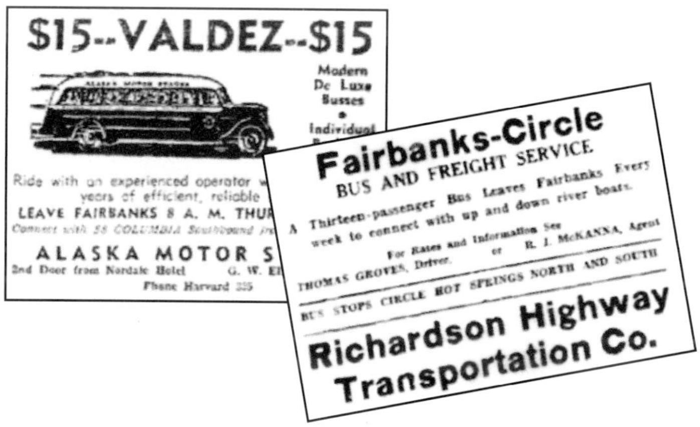

The Richardson Highway was Alaska's first long-distance road to the interior. It started as a trail to the gold camp at Eagle on the Yukon River in the late 1800s. With the 1902 gold rush in the Fairbanks area, the trail was improved to a wagon road and by 1910 it was possible to travel from Valdez to Fairbanks and by the 1920s, the road was upgraded to allow vehicle traffic and it became an important route for freight hauling to the interior. During World War II it was developed as an all-season road with bridges built across the rivers, which had been served by ferries. With extensive snowfall in the Thompson Pass area the highway was closed during the winter after the war and not opened again all year until the 1950s. Its southern terminus is the port of Valdez with a total distance of 363 miles. It is named for Major Wilde P. Richardson, a pioneer military person in the early 1900s. This photo is from 1930s. —Alaska State Library, Skinner Foundation, PCA 44-2-27

GOLDEN BELT LINE TOUR

RICHARDSON HIGHWAY . . . THRU THE GOLDEN HEART OF ALASKA

FAIRBANKS-CHITINA—317 Miles Without a Crossroad

Paxon's Lake, as Viewed From Highway

Mt. Drum From Richardson Highway

The Richardson Highway (Auto Trail) was constructed and is maintained by the U. S. War Department. Passing thru Four Mountain Ranges (Alaska, Wrangell, Talkeetna and Coast), innumerable lakes, rivers, water-falls, Indian villages, etc., it is Alaska's Wonder Trip for Tourists and Hunters. We operate the most modern cars and buses over the highway (in connection with the Golden Belt Line Tour), making the trip in three days on a set schedule that allows sufficient time for visiting points of interest, fishing, hiking, etc.

SPECIAL FEATURE FOR 1930

Midnight Sun Trip

SEE THE ALASKA RANGE AT MIDNIGHT

Continuous daylight during June and July, makes it possible to motor over the Highway on a night schedule. Parties so wishing, may do so with the same comfort as the day trip. Pictures taken at Midnight will be as clear as those taken at Midday.

RICHARDSON HIGHWAY TRANSPORTATION CO.

KNOWN BY EVERY TOURIST AGENCY IN AMERICA — **FAIRBANKS, ALASKA**

ALASKA/YUKON ROADS AND HIGHWAYS

The very scenic, 187-mile **TOP OF THE WORLD HIGHWAY** linking Dawson City with the Taylor Highway at Tok, Alaska and the Alaska Highway was completed in 1955. It was all paved in the 1990s but was never properly maintained and is mostly gravel now. The road follows around the high points of a series of ridges above timberline and is to be driven slowly and with caution. It is open from late spring to early fall, depending on weather conditions. The Little Gold-Poker Creek border crossing is the most northern US-Canada crossing in North America. When it closes—usually in September—no crossings are allowed. The little gas station and store and a few residents of Chicken is the first stop in Alaska and tours are conducted in the summer of the historic Pedro gold dredge remains in the area.

Completed in 1971, the **GEORGE PARKS HIGHWAY** (The Parks Highway, Alaska Route 3) mostly parallels the Alaska Railroad from the Glenn Highway, north of Anchorage, 323 miles to Fairbanks. It is named for George Alexander Parks, governor of the Territory of Alaska from 1925 to 1933. It provides access by motor transportation to Denali National Park and Preserve and Denali State Park, and it is the main access to the vast Matanuska-Susitna Valley. Before this highway, the only way to drive from Anchorage to Fairbanks was to drive the Glenn Highway, north and east, 189 miles to the junction with the Richardson Highway at Glennallen, then north to its intersection at Delta Junction, and then west to Fairbanks. The Alaska Highway eventually also connected at Delta Junction. The Elliott Highway, completed in 1959 connects Fairbanks, 152 miles to Manley Hot Springs with a junction at Livengood, where it connects with the Haul Road. The Tok Highway starts at Gakona, 146 miles north to its junction at Tok with the Alaska Highway.

The **DALTON HIGHWAY**, also called the Haul Road, is one of the northern-most roads in the world. The Alyeska Pipeline Service Company originally constructed the highway to support the development of the Trans-Alaska Pipeline and the oil fields on the North Slope. The 414-mile highway runs from Livengood, 80 miles north of Fairbanks to Deadhorse on the shores of the Arctic Ocean. The state now owns and maintains it. The majority of the road's use is by trucks carrying supplies north. It has become a tourist highway too, although the road is rugged and extra caution should be taken on driving it.

The **KLONDIKE HIGHWAY** is composed of two sections: the South Klondike and the North Klondike. The highway links Skagway, Alaska, at the head of The Lynn Canal, 440.2 miles to Dawson City, Yukon, with a short stretch in British Columbia. It resembles the route taken by the early prospectors heading to the Klondike Gold Rush. The first 14.4 miles in Alaska is designated Alaska-98 and the remaining 425.9 miles in the Yukon and British Columbia is Yukon Highway 2.

YUKON HIGHWAY 5 and Northwest Territories Highway 8, The Dempster Highway, is named after renowned NWMP officer William Dempster, who discovered the fate of a lost patrol in 1911. It begins 25 miles east of Dawson City and traverses primitive country, 458 miles to Inuvik, Northwest Territories. The road connects the Canadian road system with the Arctic Ocean. The road is gravel making it a long trip for anyone, especially the average tourist.

THE ALASKA/ALCAN HIGHWAY

For many years before America's entry into World War II there were proposals to construct a road link to Alaska through Canada. With the Japanese military threating the West Coast, the US Army, with Canadian consent, started a massive road building project, about 1,500 miles from Dawson Creek, British Columbia to a junction at Delta Junction, Alaska, 98 miles from Fairbanks in May 1942. Combat engineer regiments, including three of segregated black troops, started from both ends of the project, with supply points of Skagway (WP&YR), Whitehorse, and Fairbanks.

The Canol Road, another military road that started at Johnson's Crossing and headed north to Norman Wells, NWT, followed the route of the pipeline that carried oil to the refinery at Whitehorse. It is not open to motorized vehicles.

CHECK LATEST INFORMATION FOR CURRENT CONDITIONS

TWO-WAY MILEAGE TABLE, ALASKA HIGHWAY ACCOMMODATIONS

SEE TABLE OF CONTENTS FOR ROUTE TO ANCHORAGE AND OTHER MILEAGE TABLES

Miles from Dawson Creek			Miles from Fairbanks
0	—DAWSON CREEK	ALL	1520
35.5	—Taylor (PO, TT) Rainbow Motel	MLGrS	1484.5
47	—Pappy's Service & Cafe (T)	MG	1473
47.5	—Mighty Peace Motel (T)	LG	1472.5
47.8	—Fort St. John (PO, TT) Condill Hotel	MLGRS	1472.5
48	—Bedore's Motel (T)	L	1472
52	—Charlie Lake (PO, T) Motel, McMahon's Gar., Cafe	MLGRS	1468
101	—Blueberry Lodge, Cafe, Garage (PO, TT)	MLGRS	1419
136	—Black Spruce Lodge	ML	1384
146.9	—Pink Mountain Lodge (T)	MLGR	1373.1
147	—Beaton River Lodge, store (PO, T)	MLGRS	1373
171	—Mason Creek Lodge (T)	MLGR	1349
200	—Trutch Lodge (TT)	MLGS	1320
233	—Lum 'N Abner's Cabins, Cafe (T)	MLGr	1287
278.5	—Last Resort (T)	MLGr	1241.5
295.5	—Highway Auto Ser[illegible]fe, Cabins	MLGR	1224.5
300	—Fort Nelson ([illegible], TT) Ft. Nelson & Avonlee Hotels, Starlite Motel, Parkers Service, Muskwa Cafe, cabins	MLGRS	1220
351	—Steamboat Mountain Lodge	MLGR	1169
392	—Summit Lake Hotel & Garage (TT)	MLGRS	1128
397	—Rocky Mountain Auto Court (T)	MLGRS	1123
419	—Lash Callison's Big Game Guides, Outfitters		1101
422	—Toad River Lodge & Garage (T)	MLGR	1098
442	—The Village (T)	MLGS	1078
456	—Motoring Service Garage (TT)	GR	1064
462	—Highland Glen Cabins (TT)	LGS	1058
463	—Muncho Lake Lodge (TT)	MLGr	1057
463.3	—John & Marions Fishing Camp (TT)	LS	1056.7
496	—Liard River Hotel, Cabins (T)	MLGrS	1024
528	—Do Stop Inn (T)	MLG	992
533	—Coal River Lodge (T)	MLGR	987
543	—Fireside Inn (TT)	MLGr	977
596	—Iron Creek Lodge (T)	MLGrS	924
612	—Upper Liard Cafe, Cabins	MLG	908
620	—Lower Post (PO, TT, TZ) Lower Post Hotel, Cafe, Trading Post, Wright's Ranch House	MLGrS	900
633	—Straughan's "66" Services (T)	MGr	887
635	—Watson Lake (PO, TT, TZ) W. L. Hotel, Garage, Trading Post, Jac & Mac's, Sand's Store	MLGRS	885
687.3	—Transport Cafe & Rooms (T)	MLGr	832.7
710	—Rancheria Hotel (T)	MLGrS	810
733.3	—Swift River Auto Camp (PO, TT)	MLGrS	786.7
777.7	—Morley River Auto Camp (T)	MLGS	742.3
804	—Teslin Lake Motel (TT)	MLGR	716
804.5	—Teslin (PO, TT) Nisutlin Bay & T&D Stores	GS	715.5
837	—Johnson's Crossing Lodge (T)	MLGr	683
843	—Yukon Lodge (T)	MLG	677
849	—Lakeview Service	MLG	671
865.5	—Atlin Junction (Atlin, MLGrS, 60-miles)		654.5
872	—Crystal Palace Hotel & Motel (T)	MLGRS	648
883	—Marsh Lake Lodge (T)	MLGr	637
910	—McCrae Inn (T)	MLG	610
917.4	—WHITEHORSE	ALL	602.6
925.1	—Dawson-Mayo Junction (Alaska via Dawson) Mayo Hiway to Mayo, Dawson & Alaska (Takhini Hot Springs, 9.5 mi. from Jct.)		594.9
987	—Krak-R-Krik Inn (T)	MLGrS	533
996	—Canyon Creek Lodge (TT)	MLGr	524
1016	—Haines Junction (PO, TT) Haines Hwy., HJ Inn, Fairdale Store, Brewster's Lodge & Garage	MLGRS	504
1022	—Mackintosh Lodge (T)	MLGS	498
1054	—Silver Creek Lodge (T)	MLG	466
1083	—Destruction Bay Lodge (TT)	MLGS	437
1093	—Burwash Landing, Kluane Lodge (T)	MLGrS	427
1095	—Joe's Airport Lodge (T)	MLGR	425
1128	—Bradley's Mountain View Service	Gr	392
1168	—White River Lodge (T)	MLGRS	352
1202	—Beaver Creek Lodge (T)	MLG	318
1202.1	—Canada Customs & Immigration (stop)		317.9
1221	—International Boundary, Canada-Alaska TZ		299
1225.5	—Border Trading Post (T)	GS	294.5
1226	—Scotty Creek Lodge (T)	MLGR	294
1235	—Seaton's Service & Cafe (T)	MG	285
1263	—Northway Motel & Garage (T)	MLGR	257
1264	—Northway Junction (TT) 6.5 mi. to Airport		256
1281	—Riverside Lodge (T)	MLGRS	239
1301	—Tetlin Junction, Taylor Hwy. (Dawson, Eagle) Forty-Mile Roadhouse (T)	MLGR	219
1314	—Tok Junction (PO, TT) U.S. Customs & Immigration, Posts Cafe, Garage, Parker House, Tok Lodge, Gilliams Store & Glenn Highway to Anchorage	MLGRS	206
1338.5	—Cathedral Bluffs Lodge (T)	MLGS	181.5
1361.5	—Dot Lake Lodge (T)	MLGS	158.5
1385	—Halfway Inn (T)	MLG	135
1423	—Big Delta Junction (PO, TT) Richardson Hiway, Arts Tr. Post, Bays Hotel, Buffalo Lodge, LA City Limits	MLGRS	97
1452	—Richardson Roadhouse (T)	MLG	68
1469.5	—Silver Fox Lodge (T)	MLG	50.5
1475.5	—Salchaket Lodge (T)	MGS	44.5
1479.5	—Aurora Lodge (T)	MLG	40.5
1506	—North Pole Village—"Santa Claus House" (PO, TT)	MLGRS	14
1520	—FAIRBANKS	ALL	0

Symbols: ALL—All facilities (Cities, towns) M—Meals, L—Lodging, G—Gas & oil, R—Auto repairs (complete), r—minor repairs, S—Store with groceries PO—Post Office, TT—Telephone & Telegraph, T—Telephone, TZ—Time Zone (reset watches)

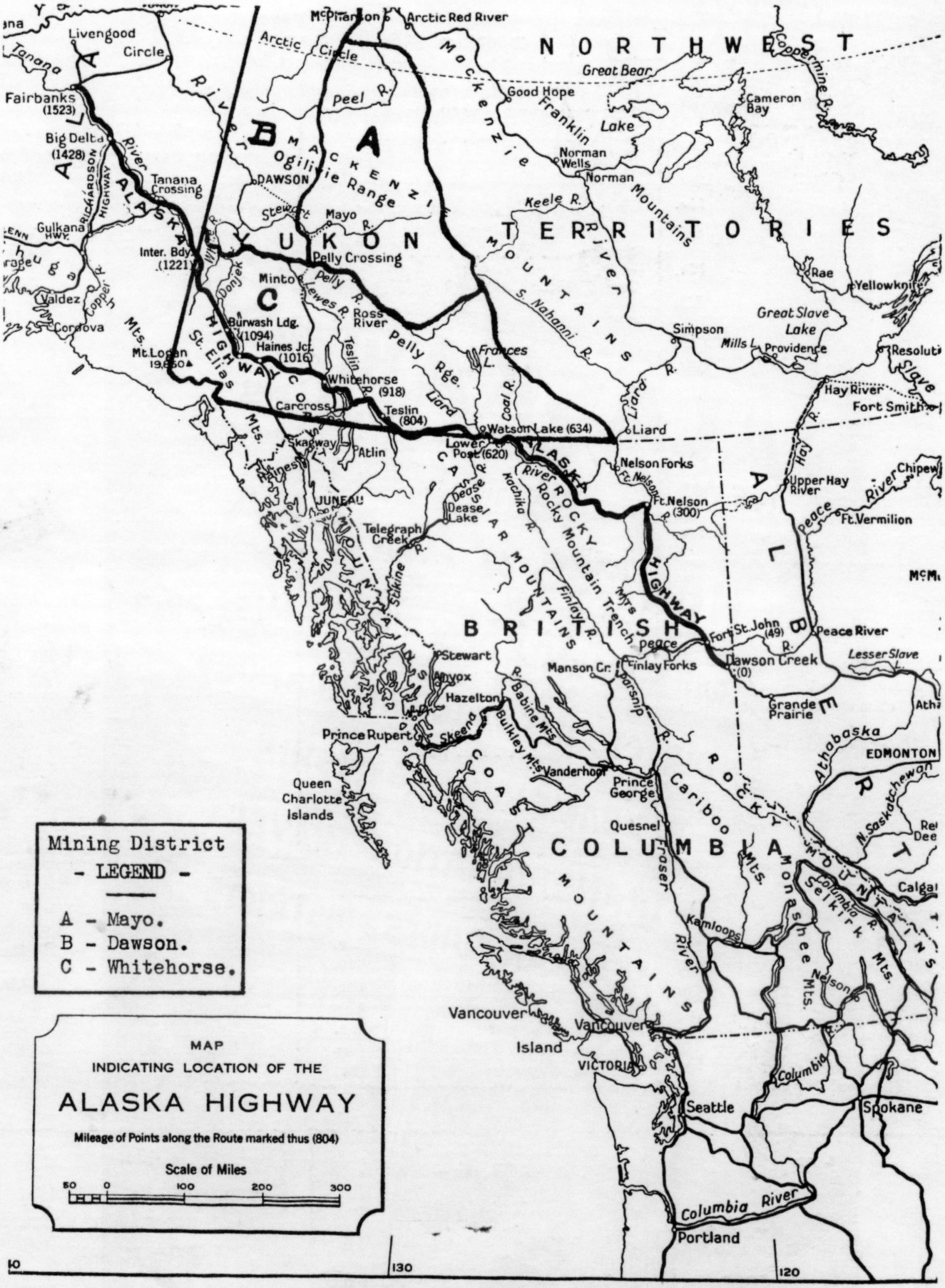

COMPLIMENTARY MENUS ON REQUEST

The first issue in 1949 of the popular guidebook, The Milepost, *now describes the Alaska Highway and roads and towns in Alaska, Yukon, Alberta and British Columbia.*

Dawson Creek, British Columbia, is the official starting point for the World War II era Alaska (ALCAN) Highway. It was selected because it was the end of rail transportation, which was important for supplying material, equipment, etc. for the highway construction and later for the CANOL pipeline and road to the oilfields at Norman Wells, Northwest Territories. —AC

Many obstacles had to be overcome in building this road including very steep grades, this one known as suicide hill. —AC

At Watson Lake, Yukon, a lonely US soldier put up a sign designating his home town. During and after the war, the site has grown to be a major tourist attraction with over 77,000 signs today. A visitor's center has been built near the site. The Cassier Highway heading due south into British Columbia starts here. —Michael Gates photo

Edmonton, Alberta, which is on the main route to Dawson Creek and was the main headquarters during the construction phase of the highway and also lays claim to the start of the highway. —AC

Liard River Lodge

(LIARD HOT SPRINGS REGION)

An ideal spot for a four-season holiday.

Make Liard River Lodge your base for enjoying the Hot Springs, hiking or exploring many miles of crosscountry trails. Afterward enjoy a hearty home-cooked meal.

Liard Hot Springs is 477 miles north of Dawson Creek and is part of Liard Hot Springs Provincial Park with a boardwalk to both Alpha and Beta pools, both with changing rooms. It is a great respite for travelers and is open year-round. Photo circa 1970s.

The highway, really only a rough dirt road, was dedicated on November 20, 1942 at Soldiers' Summit on Kluane Lake, Yukon.

Program

Invocation — Father Charles Hamel, O.M.I.
Opening Remarks — Col. K. B. Bush, G.S.C. Master of Ceremonies
Reading of Messages. Col. John W. Wheeler, C.E.
Introductions
Col. E. G. Paules - Whitehorse Sector;
Col. Robert D. Ingalls - Ft. St. John Sector;
Enlisted Men who will hold the Ribbon:
Corp. Refines Sims Jr., Pvt. Alfred Jalufka
Whitehorse Sector;
Mstr. Sgt. Andrew E. Doyle, Corp. John T. Reilly
Fort St. John Sector.
Message from the Canadian Armed Forces
Maj. Gen. George R. Pearkes.
Message from Public Roads Administration and Civilian Contractors
Mr. J.S. Bright, District Engineer.
Message from the Premier of Alberta
by Hon. W. A. Fallow
Further Reading of Messages — Col. Bush
Remarks — Dr. Charles Camsell, Commissioner Northwest Territories
Introduction of Insp. William Grennan, R.C.M.P.
Speech for Dominion of Canada and Reading of Message from the Prime Minister by Hon. Ian Mackenzie
Speech for Territory of Alaska and Reading of Message from the Governor by Hon. E.L. Bartlett
Response on behalf of the American Army.
Brig. Gen. James A. O'Connor, commanding N.W. Serv. Command
Cutting of Ribbon — Mr. Mackenzie, Mr. Bartlett
"GOD SAVE THE KING" - "THE STAR SPANGLED BANNER"
U.S. Army Bands
Benediction — Capt. Ervin T. May, Chaplain, U.S.A.

DEDICATION
KLUANE LAKE - YUKON -
NOVEMBER - 20TH - 1942.

Menu

SUPPER
Thursday, November 19, 1942, 6 PM

ST. ELIAS MOUNTAIN SHEEP
Nosheep Brown Gravy
Spinach à la Kloo - Takhini Corn
Tanana Potatoes
SLIMS RIVER SALAD
Chisana Apple Sauce - Siwash Gelatin
Coffee à la Yukon
China-Way Tea
Moose Milk
Sour Dough Bread - Bull-Dozer Butter

BREAKFAST
Friday, November 20, 7:15 AM

Burwash Prunes
Grapefruit Juice - Alcan - Tomato Juice
Alberta Farina
Aishihik Sausage - Dezadeash Eggs
Toast - Butter
Coffee - Sugar - Milk

DINNER
Friday, November 20, 12 Noon

CHAMPAGNE SOUP
MOOSE STEAK à la Donjek
Pickhandle Beans - Kaskawulsh Potatoes
Nabesna Peas and Carrots
KLUANE SALAD
HORSE CAMP PUDDING
Dawson Creek Crackers - Fairbanks Cheese
1630 Miles Coffee
Tea - Orange Juice - Milk
Bread - Butter

COMMITTEE: Col. T. W. Essig, Maj. R.C. Luckow, Maj. E. W. Stann, Capt. P.L. Reed, Capt. R. A. Johnson, Lt. F. C. Bishop, Lt. B. B. Miller, Lt. R.L. Neuberger.

—Jeff Stevens collection

Roll North Over The

ALASKA HIGHWAY

in Luxurious New B.Y.N. Busses

New B. Y. N. "Pony Cruiser" bus, seating 20 passengers.

When Your Bus Reaches Whitehorse There Are Inviting Side-trips to Take

1. For a complete change of pace, sail down the Yukon River, aboard a B. Y. N. steamer, to the Klondike and Dawson City. The round trip takes about a week and is a perfect contrast to your bus ride, giving you a chance to re-live the colorful gold-rush days of '98.

2. For an indescribably glamorous experience, take the train to Carcross for the overnight steamer trip to Ben-My-Chree, the former home of a romantic couple who found supreme happiness in this wilderness of glacier-mantled mountains mirrored in glassy blue lakes.

3. For a thrill-packed day, ride the White Pass & Yukon Railroad all the way down to Skagway, a 110 mile trip during which the perilous first leg of the "Trail of '98" can be plainly traced through your parlour-car window. (*Those wishing to return home via the Inside Passage may make southbound steamer connections at Skagway for Seattle or Vancouver.*)

On to Alaska

The bus trip over the rest of the Alaska Highway, from Whitehorse to Fairbanks, takes two days and includes an overnight stop at the White Pass & Yukon lodge at Dry Creek. From Fairbanks, among other things, you can fly to Nome; visit Circle Hot Springs; go by rail to McKinley National Park and Anchorage; or continue by bus over the Richardson Highway to Anchorage.

Airplane connections may also be made at Whitehorse for practically any point in Alaska.

The Best Time to Go

B. Y. N. busses operate throughout the year, but those traveling solely for pleasure will probably find the period from late May through September most enjoyable. Temperatures at this time range between 60 and 80 degrees.

Your travel agent will gladly help you plan your trip. Or write to:

Swift, Regular "Pony Cruiser" Service
to the Heart of America's Last Frontier
Operated by the White Pass & Yukon Route

F. G. DOWNEY
General Agent
W. P. & Y. Route
17 Commerce Building
Vancouver, B. C.

J. G. BLANCHARD
General Passenger Agent
W. P. & Y. Route
P. O. Box 1846
Seattle 11, Wash.

FORM P-23

LITHOGRAPHED IN U.S.

TRIP ON THE ALCAN BY JEFF STEVENS OF MISSOULA, MONTANA

This is a somewhat tattered Milepost Guidebook used by the Stevens family on their 1953 journey from Missoula, Montana, to Fairbanks and Anchorage on the ALCAN Highway. They covered about 5,500 miles over challenging roads in July and August of 1953.

The travelers consisted of father John, wife Esther, children Pat, Jeff and Nancy, and Esther's sister Patsy in addition to a very large German Shepherd named Ted. They were all crammed into a 1951 Oldsmobile 98 towing a '40s vintage canned ham travel trailer.

Jeff, though four at the time, had vivid memories of the route being lined with thousands of blown out tires. They suffered only two flat tires on the trip, one on the car and one on the trailer. On one occasion, a southbound traveler told them the road ahead was terrible and urged them to turn back, but they proceeded on.

The route was mostly dirt, gravel, and mud. One day a rear section of sheet metal on the trailer came loose, dragging on the gravel for miles and filling the trailer with dust.

When they came to the Chistochina River the water was raging and the bridge was shaking. They crossed safely. A couple days later, newspapers reported that the bridge had collapsed shortly after they had crossed. It was replaced before their return trip.

The landscape was vast and spectacular, and the mosquitos were numerous and huge. The biting No See Ums were small enough to pass through any screen. South of Fairbanks, Pat dropped the last roll of toilet paper in a creek. John made him hold it out the window to dry out as they traveled on. When they entered Fairbanks, people were laughing and pointing at the car. Pat was still holding the toilet paper out of the window.

The 1951 Oldsmobile and trailer.

Left to right: Patsy, Jeff, John and Pat Stevens.

The pioneer road had been punched through in record time, a little over eight months. In early 1943 the US Public Roads Administration had the job of upgrading the road to year-round passable use. Grades had to be reduced and straightened, new roadbeds had to be built across the many swampy sections, and permanent bridges were built to replace the temporary ones. Both American and Canadian companies worked on the upgrade. The total cost of the road was over $138 million and required the placement of 133 bridges and 8,000 culverts. The military road was turned over to the Canadians in early 1946 and soon to the Royal Canadian Army. The road opened to civilian traffic on a full-time basis in 1949 and the road has been greatly improved through the years and is maintained by both countries in their respective territories.

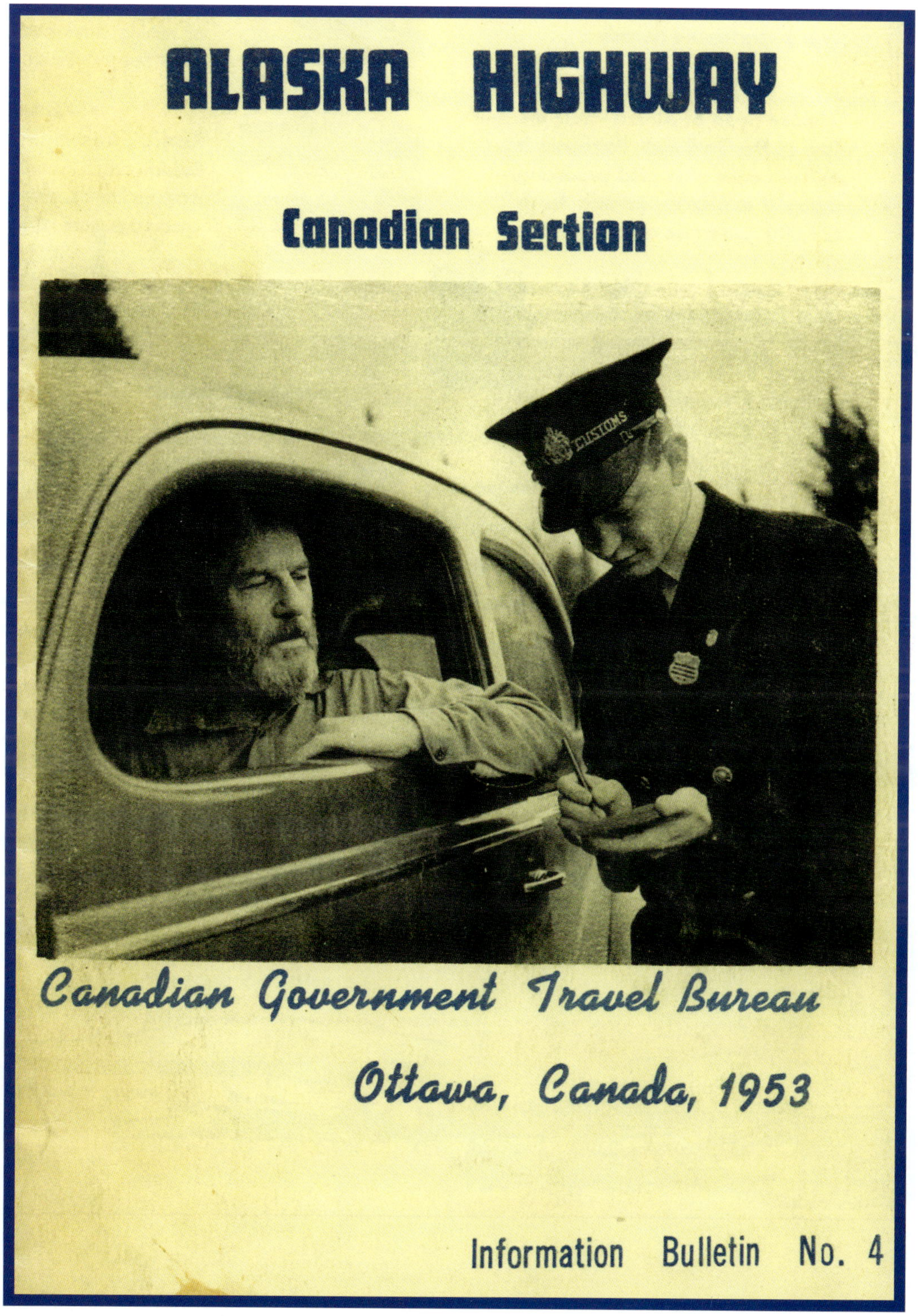

cities and towns

JUNEAU—Beautifully situated, Alaska's capital is in the center of a rich fishing region. Tourists find the area a sportsman's paradise.

FAIRBANKS—Called the "Golden Heart of Alaska" from the days of the Gold Rush, Fairbanks is still the center of a gold producing region. It is also the junction for a 227,000 mile trade area.

ANCHORAGE—Alaska's most rapidly growing city is headquarters for the government-owned Alaska Railroad. It is in the heart of Alaska's agricultural region and the site of mammoth construction projects.

SITKA—Once the capital of Russian America, Sitka is picturesque with remnants of Czarist occupation. Fishing supports more than half the population. Also site of Pioneer's Home and Sheldon Jackson Museum.

SEWARD—is the chief port of southwestern Alaska and is located at the head of the spectacular Kenai Peninsula where sportsmen find some of the world's finest fishing.

WRANGELL—Famous for totems and Indian lore, is another fishing center. Proximity to Tongass National Forest has led to a sawmill and box factory with further lumber development expected.

SKAGWAY—This breaking point between water and land transportation was a resting place for Klondike miners and is rich with tales of mining days and Alaska's fabulous "Soapy" Smith.

KODIAK—Established in 1791, Kodiak has many traces of its Russian origin in contrast with today's modern homes, civic enterprises and encouragement of new industries.

NOME—Best known for its colorful gold rush history and for its nearly 24 hours of summer daylight, Nome also serves as headquarters for Alaska's Second Judicial Division.

KETCHIKAN—This colorful city is the center for southeastern Alaska's fishermen. It is also first port of call for visitors who include modern canneries in their sightseeing tours.

PETERSBURG—Known for its beautiful harbor and mountain scenery, Petersburg is near Leconte Glacier which drops thousands of icebergs into the water each year. Fishing and fur farming are the chief industries.

CORDOVA—Salmon, crab and clam canneries, together with herring packing provide important industries for Cordova. Headquarters for Chugach National Forest, Cordova is unsurpassed for scenic beauty.

On our way to ALASKA
SOUTHERN PACIFIC LINES

ALASKA FOR AN AIR-COOLED VACATION
THE ALASKA LINE
ALASKA STEAMSHIP CO.
CHICAGO MILWAUKEE ST. PAUL AND PACIFIC
Route of The Olympian

THE TRIANGLE TOUR OF BRITISH COLUMBIA
ALASKA
AND THE YUKON
1929
CANADIAN NATIONAL
Largest Railway System in America
CANADIAN NATIONAL
Largest Railway System in America

The Klondike Mines Railway ran 31 miles from Klondike City to Kings Dome. It started in 1906 to haul supplies and passengers to the dredge and hydraulic operations. It ceased operation in 1914. The Seward Peninsula is now part of the Alaska Railroad; the Copper River & Northwestern Railroad is no longer in business; the White Pass & Yukon Route is now a very popular narrow-gauge, tourist railroad in the summer season; the Canadian National Railroad is Canada's largest and started in 1918 and with a merger with several US railroads it serves Canada and parts of the US and Mexico with freight hauling. the Northern Alberta Railroad started in 1929 and merged with the Canadian National Railroad in 1981. The railroad's museum is located in McLennan, Alberta.

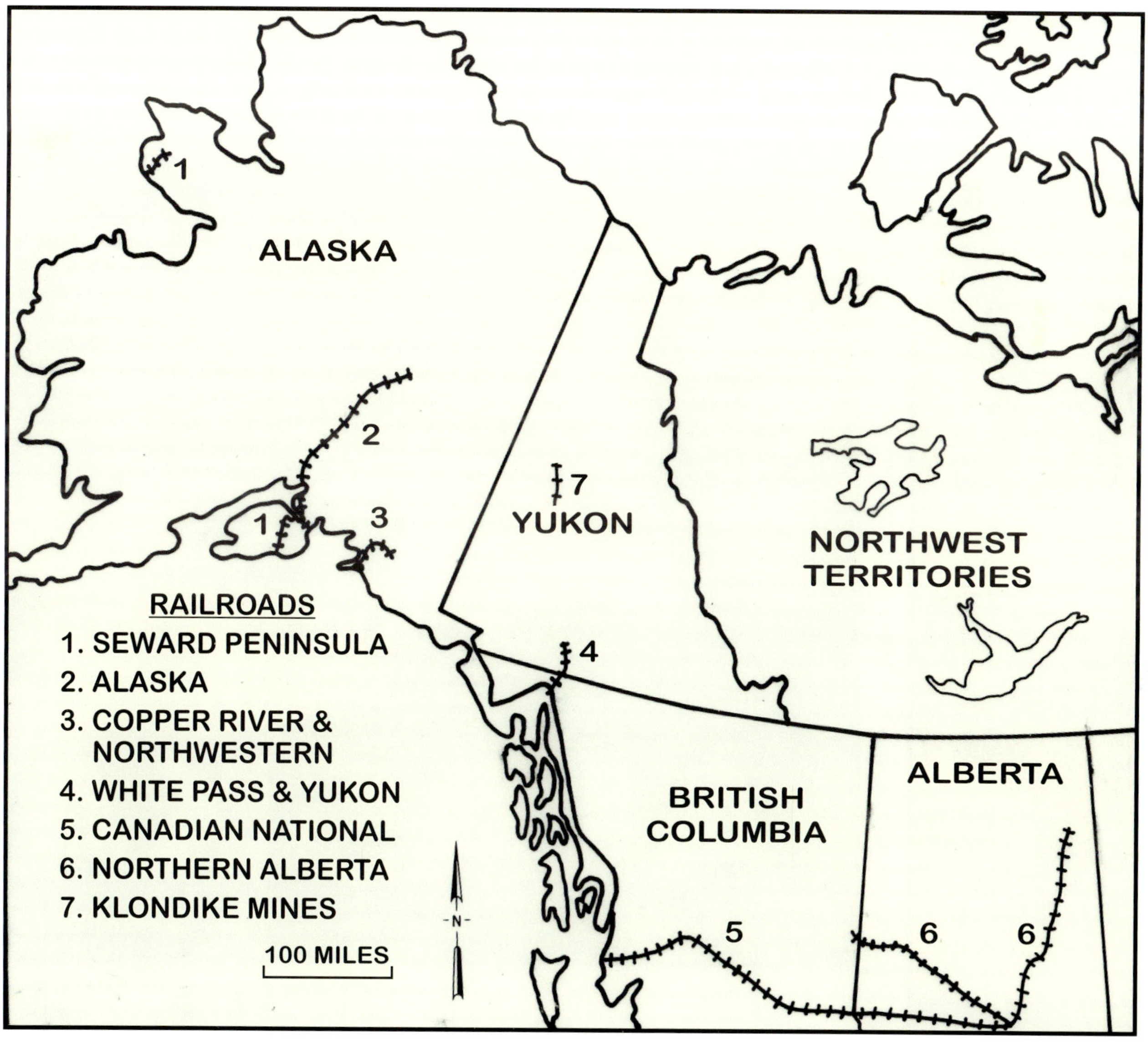

ALASKA
VIA
NORTHERN PACIFIC
R.R.

BETWEEN
CHICAGO and PACIFIC NORTHWEST
GREAT NORTHERN RAILWAY
Visit
GLACIER NATIONAL PARK
Route of the
EMPIRE
BUILDER
THE OHIO MATCH CO. WADSWORTH, OHIO
MADE IN U.S.A.

ALASKA
CANADIAN NATIONAL RAILWAYS

THE ALASKA RAILROAD

Like the transcontinental railroads of the American West, the Alaska Railroad opened up vast frontiers for settlement. It was completed in 1923 and spawned towns along its route. It is and probably will remain, the last of the major rail lines to be hacked out of the North American wilderness.

The railroad is a vital part of Alaska's economy. Not only does it handle thousands of goods between the coast and the interior, it also takes tourists and other travelers through some of the most beautiful scenery in the world.

Unlike most of the nation's railroads, the Alaska Railroad was totally financed and constructed by the US Government. Construction began in 1914 at the time of the completion of the Panama Canal. Although the projects were separated by thousands of miles, the railroad and the canal shared some of the same supervisory personnel and equipment, and both opened up major commercial arteries.

Several existing small railroads were purchased at the start of construction including the Alaska Central Railroad out of Seward, renamed and refinanced as the Alaska Northern Railway Company in 1908 and the 44.7 mile narrow-gauge, Tanana Valley Railroad out of Fairbanks. The final link was in 1923 with the completion of the Mears Memorial Bridge across the Tanana

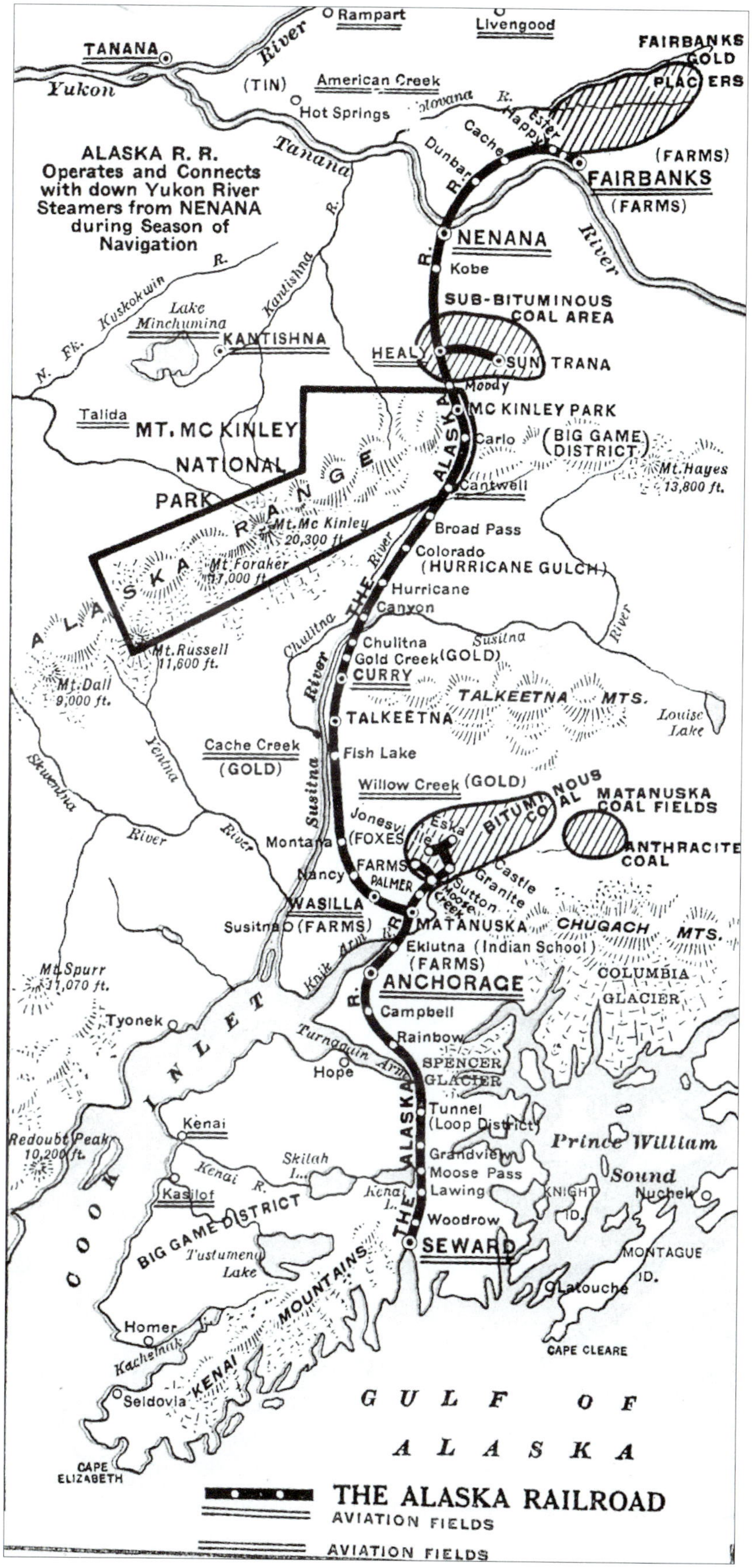

An older map of the railroad.

—AC

River at Nenana. The Golden Spike Ceremony was held on July 16, 1923 at the north end of the bridge with President Warren G. Harding driving the golden spike.

One can also draw an analogy between the construction of the railroad and the building of the Alyeska oil pipeline in the mid-twentieth century. Both were built at great cost and difficulty and both were built to transport goods or natural resources through the wilds of America's last frontier.

The 470-mile railroad has done as much for Alaska as any other single project in the state's history. Anchorage came into being as a result of the railroad and Fairbanks, which started out early in the century as a booming gold-rush town became the northern terminus. Seward, at the railroad's southern terminus, took on tremendous importance at the onset of construction.

At the start of America's entry into World War II the railroad was guarded by civilian guards but in 1943 the US Army took it over and operated it until May 1945 when it was returned to the Federal Government. During this time, maintenance was improved, new equipment added, a bypass was built around the famous "loop," and a spur was built, including a tunnel to the ice-free port of Whittier.

The tourist business did not form a significant portion of the railroad's revenues until after the war. Airlines and the Alaska Highway added significant numbers of people who wanted to visit the area. Before this time, it took three to six weeks to make a tour and accommodations were limited. Two hotels owned by the railroad, the Curry Hotel and The McKinley Park Hotel, had been built in 1923 and 1939 respectively and McKinley Park was the main attraction for visitors to ride the train.

During the 1964 Good Friday earthquake, the railroad and the Port of Whitter along with Seward and Valdez suffered major damage.

In January 1985, the state bought the railroad from the US Government and operates it today for passengers and freight. In 2005, five luxury dome cars with dining cars were added for the tourist trade.

BIG GAME HUNTING
ALONG THE
ALASKA RAILROAD
U.S. Department of the Interior
THE ALASKA RAILROAD
Interior Alaska Line
Mt. McKinley National Park Route

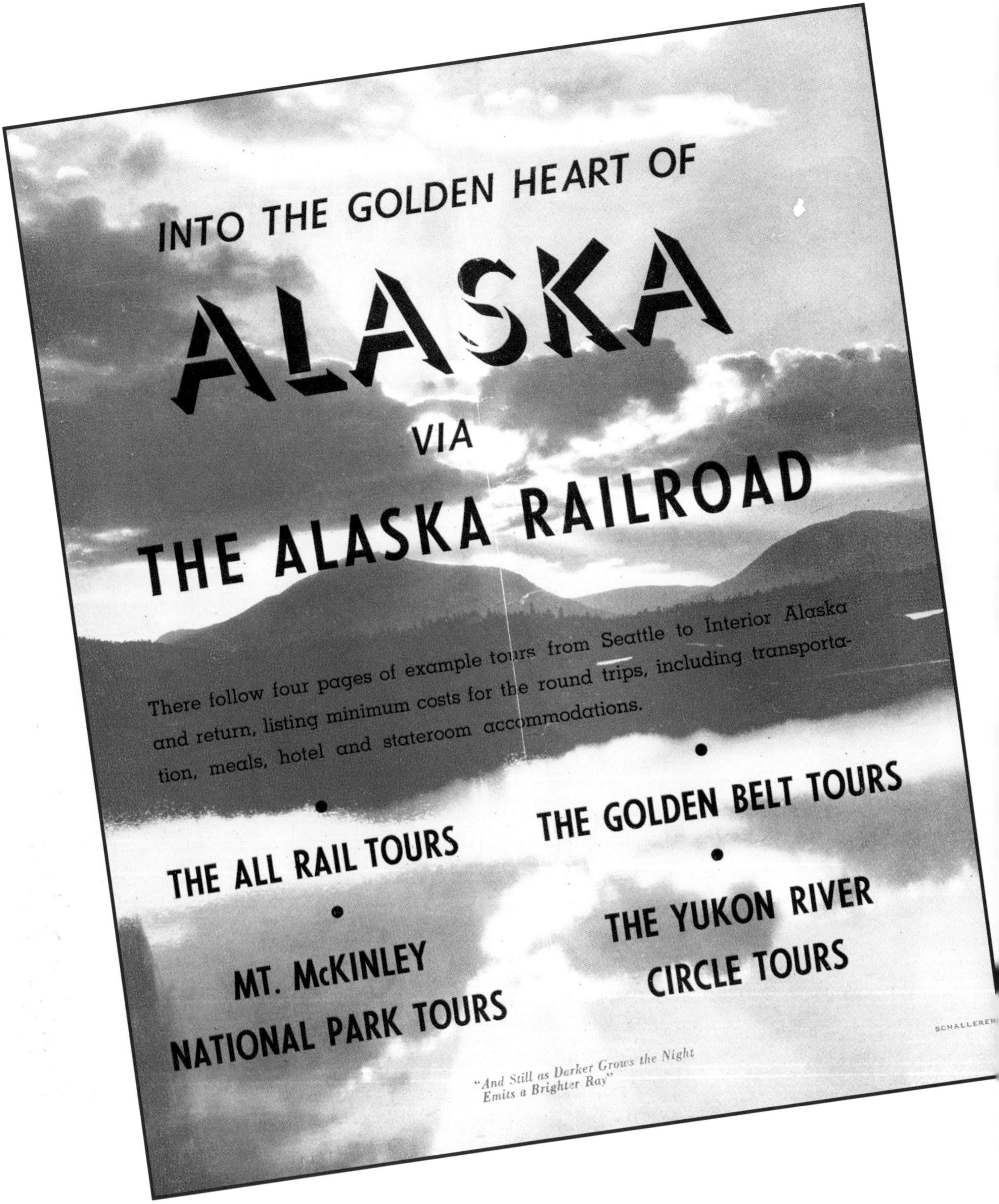
INTO THE GOLDEN HEART OF
ALASKA
VIA
THE ALASKA RAILROAD
There follow four pages of example tours from Seattle to Interior Alaska and return, listing minimum costs for the round trips, including transportation, meals, hotel and stateroom accommodations.
THE ALL RAIL TOURS
MT. McKINLEY NATIONAL PARK TOURS
THE GOLDEN BELT TOURS
THE YUKON RIVER CIRCLE TOURS
"And Still as Darker Grows the Night Emits a Brighter Ray"
SCHALLERER

ALASKA
THE ALASKA RAILROAD
Mt. McKinley Park Route
ALASKA
from Sheltered Seas
to Golden Heart
VIA THE ALASKA RAILROAD
U.S. Department of the Interior
THE ALASKA RAILROAD
Interior Alaska Line
Mt. McKinley National Park Route
U.S. DEPARTMENT OF THE INTERIOR
THE ALASKA RAILROAD
Mt. McKinley Park Route

The "ALL RAIL TOUR"

Sailings from Seattle to Seward every Saturday and Wednesday at 9:00 a. m.

Interior Alaska via The Alaska Railroad

19 Days — Seattle to Interior Alaska and return

EXAMPLE ITINERARY

McKinley Park Season—June 10 to September 15

1st Day, SATURDAY—Leave Seattle by steamship 9:00 a.m. Steam northward through Puget Sound and Canadian waters.

2nd Day, SUNDAY—Cruising through Canadian waters of the Inside Passage, between Vancouver Island and the mainland.

3rd Day, MONDAY—Steamer crosses the International Boundary (54° 40′), enters American waters, makes calls at Ketchikan and Wrangell.

4th Day, TUESDAY—Still cruising, northward, through the Inside Passage. Call at Juneau, Alaska's "Capital City," where sufficient time is allowed for visit to the Territorial Museum and for an automobile trip to Auk Lake and Mendenhall Glacier.

5th Day, WEDNESDAY—Crossing the Gulf of Alaska; Malaspina Glacier, largest in the world, may be observed. Arrive Cordova during the evening. The steamer continues its cruise through Prince William Sound, making calls at Valdez and Columbia Glacier.

NOTE: Saturday sailings make stops at Valdez and Cordova when southbound only.

6th Day, THURSDAY—Arrive Seward in the morning; leave at 9:00 a.m. for the Interior, via The Alaska Railroad, arriving Anchorage 1:55 p.m. Headquarters: Hotel Anchorage or Hotel Parsons. Time in Anchorage allows for side trip by automobile to Lake Spenard Bathing Resort and around the Loop Highway.

NOTE: Travelers may spend the day sightseeing in Seward and vicinity, leaving Friday at 7:30 a.m. for the Interior; lunch at Anchorage, and departure at 2:00 p.m. for Curry.

7th Day, FRIDAY—Continuing northward trip by rail, leave Anchorage 10:00 a.m., arrive Palmer 11:59 a.m.; leave Palmer 3:00 p.m. and connect with main line train at Matanuska for Curry. Arrive Curry 6:30 p.m. for dinner and overnight stop at Curry Hotel.

NOTE: Those who do not desire to make the Palmer side trip may remain in Anchorage until 2:00 p.m.

8th Day, SATURDAY—Leave Curry 7:45 a.m. Arrive McKinley Park 11:40 a.m. Headquarters: Mt. McKinley National Park Hotel, at Park entrance. Motor trips listed below.

9th Day, SUNDAY—In McKinley Park.

10th Day, MONDAY—Leave McKinley Park. Continue rail trip northward at 12:25 p.m. Arrive Fairbanks 4:50 p.m. Headquarters at either Pioneer or Nordale Hotel.

11th Day, TUESDAY—In Fairbanks; side trips to the following places may be made by automobile—the University of Alaska, U. S. Agricultural Experiment Station, flower gardens, and the placer and dredge gold mining operations.

12th Day, WEDNESDAY—At 8:00 a.m. begin return trip to the coast via The Alaska Railroad; stop at McKinley Park for lunch, arrive Curry 5:15 p.m.; dinner and overnight stay at the Curry Hotel.

13th Day, THURSDAY—Continue southward journey by rail, leaving Curry 7:30 a.m. Stop at Anchorage for lunch. Arrive Seward 6:30 p.m. and, following dinner and perhaps a little sightseeing, board steamer and begin the return trip to Seattle—through Prince William Sound, Gulf of Alaska, and the Inside Passage. During the return journey the steamer will again make calls at the ports visited on the northward trip.

20th Day, THURSDAY—Steamer should dock at Seattle late in the morning or early in the afternoon.

SAILINGS

In connection with the "All Rail" Tour there are sailings from Seattle each Saturday and Wednesday at 9:00 a.m.

NOTE: For passengers leaving Seattle on Wednesday, arriving Seward on Tuesday:

7th Day, TUESDAY—Arrive Seward in the morning, leave at 7:30 a.m. for the Interior via The Alaska Railroad, arrive Anchorage at 11:59 a.m. Leave Anchorage at 2:00 p.m. Arrive Curry 6:30 p.m. for dinner and overnight stop at Curry Hotel.

8th Day, WEDNESDAY—Leave Curry 7:45 a.m. Arrive McKinley Park 11:40 a.m. Headquarters: Mt. McKinley National Park Hotel, at Park entrance. Motor trips shown below.

9th Day, THURSDAY—In Mt. McKinley National Park.

10th Day, FRIDAY—Leave McKinley Park at 12:25 p.m., arriving Fairbanks at 4:50 p.m. Headquarters: Pioneer or Nordale Hotel.

11th Day, SATURDAY—In Fairbanks; side trips may be made by automobile as follows: The University of Alaska, U. S. Agricultural Experiment Station, flower gardens, and the placer and dredge gold mining operations; also to the Circle Hot Springs and Circle City on the Steese Highway, 160 miles north of Fairbanks.

13th Day, MONDAY—At 8:00 a.m. begin return trip to the coast via The Alaska Railroad; stop at McKinley Park for lunch, arrive Curry 5:15 p.m.—dinner and overnight stay at the Curry Hotel.

14th Day, TUESDAY—Leave Curry 7:20 a.m., arrive Anchorage 11:50 a.m. Leave Anchorage 1:30 p.m., arrive Seward 6:30 p.m.; board steamer, departing at 7:30 p.m. via one or two Prince William Sound canneries, thence the Inside Passage to Seattle.

COSTS

Steamship fare Seattle to Seward and return, minimum, including transportation, meals and stateroom accommodations	$140.00
Rail fare, Seward to Fairbanks and return	56.40
Side trip, Matanuska to Palmer and return	.55
Hotel rooms and meals in Alaska that are not included in above (estimated)	45.00
	$241.95

MT. McKINLEY NATIONAL PARK TRIPS

Trip No. 1—From new hotel to Camp Eielson and return; total distance 132 miles. Round-trip fare.......$20.00
(Possible in connection with all 24-hour stops at Park.)

Trip No. 2—From new hotel to Camp Eielson and return, including side trip, Eielson to Wonder Lake; total distance 170 miles. Round-trip fare.......27.50
(Possible in connection with 48-hour stops at Park.)

McKinley Park Hotel—Double room with bath $7.50, without bath 6.50; single room with bath $5.00, without bath $4.00.

Camp Eielson—Lodging $2.00 per person per night; breakfast, lunch, dinner, $2.00 each.

Other Trips—Other Special trips, both by auto and horseback, may be arranged for by contacting company agent at hotel.

NOTE: None of the above side trips from the Park hotel into Mt. McKinley National Park include meals and lodging.

The "GOLDEN BELT TOUR"

Interior Alaska via The Alaska Railroad and Richardson Auto Trail

Sailing from Seattle to Seward every Saturday and Wednesday at 9:00 a. m.

19 Days — Seattle to Interior Alaska and return

EXAMPLE ITINERARY

McKinley Park Season—June 10 to September 15

1st Day, SATURDAY—Leave Seattle by steamship 9:00 a.m. Steam northward through Pugent Sound and Canadian waters.

2nd Day, SUNDAY—Cruising through Canadian waters of the Inside Passage, between Vancouver Island and the mainland.

The most expensive and difficult bridge project on the railroad was the construction of a span across Hurricane Gulch at Mile 281.4. An aerial tramway had to be strung across the gulch, and construction was undertaken from both sides. It was completed in the fall of 1921. Eight and one/half miles of the 470 mainline tracks were spanned by bridges. The other two big bridge projects spanned The Susitna and Tanana rivers. —AC

During the war the railroad built a 12-mile spur to the port of Whitter by constructing a line through a 2.5-mile tunnel to the ice-free port to relieve the bottleneck of supplies at the port of Seward. In 1960 the Army deactivated its mission at the port and today Whitter is a major tourist stop with cruise ships calling there and many tours of the Portage Glacier; the Alaska Wildlife Conservation Center and other attractions. The tunnel has been renamed the Anton Anderson Memorial Tunnel, the second longest in North America. Anderson was the chief engineer on construction of the railroad and also mayor of Anchorage. In 1999 the tunnel was opened to vehicular traffic and the rail shuttle between Portage and Whitter was discontinued. The one-way tunnel is shared by the railroad and vehicle traffic with altered times of travel both ways. —AC

The new depot and general office for the railroad at Anchorage was opened in 1942. The old depot, shown at left (top photo) was soon removed. In 1992 a new headquarters building was built along Ship Creek. Engine No. 1, built in 1902 sits on a pedestal as shown on the right. It hauled dirt for the Panama Canal construction and freight on the Alaska Railroad until 1953. A new depot/office has been built. —AC

The Alaska Central Railroad started a rail project in 1903 heading north. Between mile 47 and 53, the route had to cross a high point in the Kenai Mountains and avoid the path of two glaciers. This became known as the Loop District and Tunnel No. 1, and a high trestle had to be built to allow the steam engines to make the grade starting in 1906. The entire railroad was incorporated into the new Alaska Railroad in 1914. In 1951 the railroad relocated the route around the Loop District. The Bartlett Glacier had retreated and the Loop became obsolete. There is daily passenger service from May 15 to September 25 to and from Anchorage along what is considered one of the most scenic part of the entire railroad. —AC

1920 Menu.

BUFFET CAR, A. E. C.

MENU

Oranges - .25 Bananas - .25 Apple Sauce - .25 Baked Apples - .35
Peaches - .35 Grapes - .35 Pears - .35 Grape Fruit - .35

BREAKFAST FOODS

Uncle Sam Breakfast Food - .25; Krumbles - 25; Shredded Wheat - .25
Post Toasties - .25
Grape-Nuts - .25 Corn Flakes - .25 Puffed Rice - .20 Dry Toast - .20
Buttered Toast - .20 — Dipped Toast - .20 Snails - .20 Doughnuts - .20
Drop Cakes - .20 Coffee Cake - .20 Apple turn-over - .20 Hot Buns - .20
Bread and Butter - .20 French Toast and Preserves - 1.00 Jelly - .25
Preserves or Jam - .25

DISHES COOKED TO ORDER

Ham and Eggs	$1 00	Bacon and Eggs	$1 00
Fried Ham	1 00	Fried Bacon	1 00
Minced Ham and Eggs	1 00	Ham Omelet	1 00
Bacon Omelet	1 00	Onion Omelet	1 00
Jelly Omelet	1 00	Tomato Omelet	1 00
Spanish Omelet	1 25	Oyster Omelet	1 25
Fried Eggs (3)	1 00	Shirred Eggs (3)	1 00
Fried Eggs (2)	75	Shirred Eggs (2)	75
Scrambled Eggs (2)	75	Plain Omelet	1 00
Scrambled Eggs (3)	1 00	Cheese Omelet	1 00

WE SERVE STRICTLY FRESH EGGS

Coffee Per Cup - .10 Chocolate - .15 Cocoa - .15 Pot Tea - .25
Pot of Fresh Made Coffee - .25
Matanuska Fried Potatoes to Order - .15

" WE BUY THE BEST "

Cigars — Cigarettes Fruits, Candies and Nuts.

BREAKFAST 8 A. M. to 9:30 A. M. LUNCHEON 11 to 2 P. M.

DINNER 4:30 To

J. CASY McDANNEL,
Contractor

Engine #1514 approaching the Tanana River in 1974. —AC

Lima 2-8-0 locomotive, purchased from the US Army in 1942. After being put into service, the "500" series was renumbered with 400-series designations. —AC

A view of the new Fairbanks station. It replaced the Tanana Valley Railroad station. Fairbanks is the northern terminus for the railroad's Denali Star and Aurora Winter Train. Inside is a very detailed model railroad display (The Tanana Valley Model Railroad) and gift shop. —Explore Fairbanks.com

The passenger cars Nenana and Chugach in the 1930s that hauled tourists on the railroad. —AC

Tourists boarding the train at the Denali Park station. No date. —AC

A bus waiting for tourists in 1938 when Denali National Park was first named, Mount McKinley National Park. —AC

A 1922 photo of a passenger train at Nenena. Note the observation car with its observation platform that made for an interesting ride in good weather. —AC

The Seward station in 1936 at the southern terminus of the railroad. —AC

An imposing photo of Diesel engine 1508. Notice that the logo states McKinley National Park Route instead of Mount McKinley. The railroad's first diesel locomotive was put into service in 1944 and the last steam engine was retired in 1966. —AC

UNITED STATES
DEPARTMENT OF THE INTERIOR
RAY LYMAN WILBUR, SECRETARY
NATIONAL PARK SERVICE
HORACE M. ALBRIGHT, DIRECTOR

CIRCULAR OF GENERAL INFORMATION REGARDING

MOUNT McKINLEY NATIONAL PARK ALASKA

COURTESY ALASKA RAILROAD

MOUNT McKINLEY AND REFLECTION

SEASON FROM JUNE 10 TO SEPTEMBER 15
1931

An early view of the entrance to Mount McKinley National Park. —AC

Circa, 1929.

MOUNT McKINLEY NATIONAL PARK

Mt. McKinley, the highest mountain on the North American Continent—the highest mountain in the world above its base, and an abundance of wild animal life, are the distinctive attractions of this, Uncle Sam's newest playground and second in size National Park.

Alaska White Mountain Sheep . . . Moose . . . Caribou . . . Grizzly Bear . . . Massive Glaciers . . . Rugged Mountain Scenery . . . Comfortable Accommodations . . . Good Saddle Horses . . . Experienced Guides and Packers . . . Fishing in Park . . . Hunting in Adjacent Territory.

Entrance at McKinley Park Station, Alaska Railroad, by automobile 12 miles to Savage River Camp and 40 miles to Sable Pass.

MT. McKINLEY TOURIST AND TRANSPORTATION COMPANY

Licensed Concessionaires

McKINLEY PARK, ALASKA

THE CURRY HOTEL

The building started out as a maintenance section station but turned into a hotel in 1923 as an ideal location for travelers and railroad workers. It was named for Charles F. Curry, a congressman from California, who was a strong advocate for the Alaska Railroad. It was billed as "A Palace in the Wilderness where Accommodations are Modern, Inviting and Comfortable and the Cuisine of highest order." Besides the hotel a 537-foot suspension bridge was built over the Susitna River and a shelter house to view Mount McKinley. On July 18, 1926 a fire destroyed the engine house and power plant and equipment and again in 1933 and in 1946 there was a boiler explosion. In 1926 a two-story annex was built and a golf course, tennis court and swimming pool added. There was another extension in 1935–36. In 1957, a ski hut and slopes were added but on April 9, 1957 a fire destroyed the entire complex, killing three people.

—AC

Staff of the Curry Hotel outside the entrance. —Alaska Stzte Library and Historical Collections

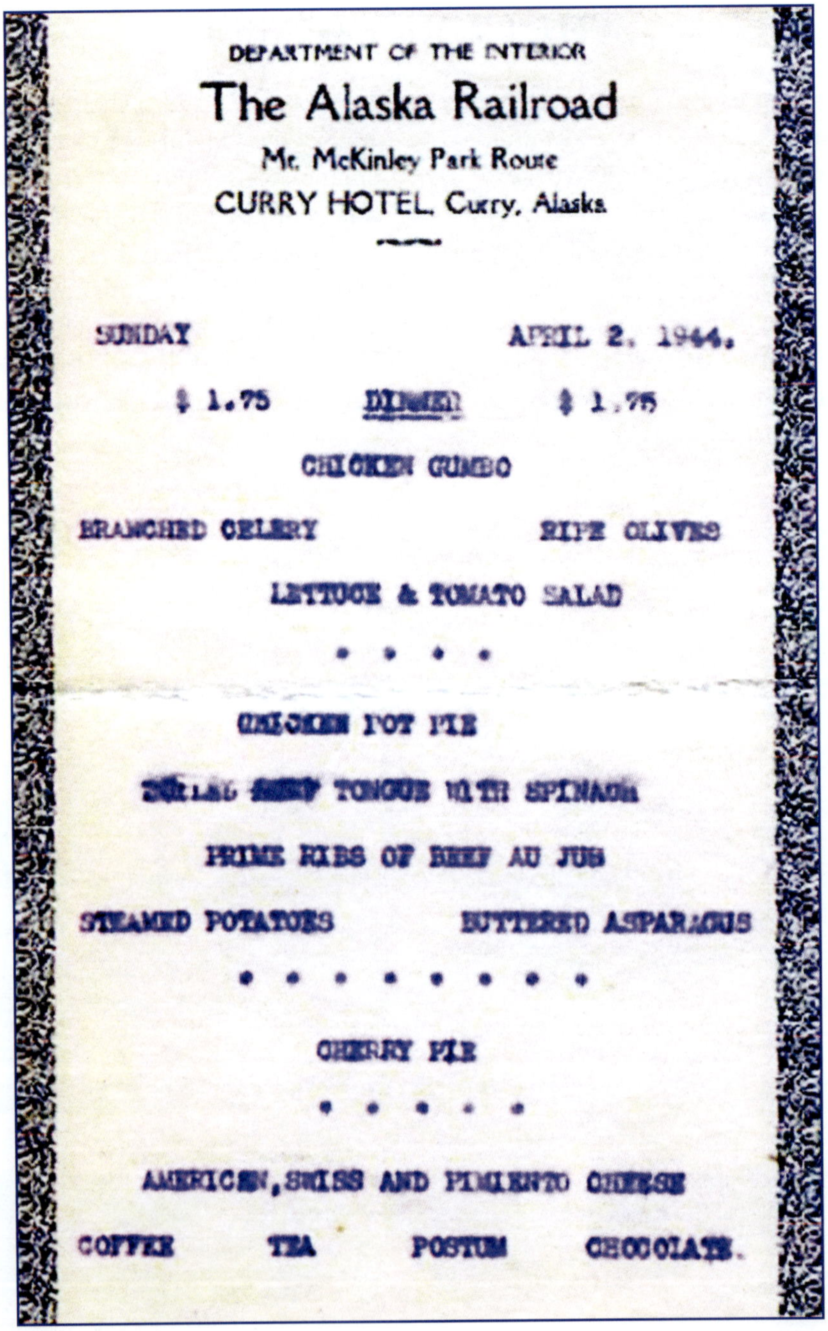
DEPARTMENT OF THE INTERIOR

The Alaska Railroad

Mt. McKinley Park Route

CURRY HOTEL, Curry, Alaska

SUNDAY APRIL 2, 1944.

$ 1.75 DINNER $ 1.75

CHICKEN GUMBO

BRANCHED CELERY RIPE OLIVES

LETTUCE & TOMATO SALAD

* * * *

CHICKEN POT PIE

BOILED BEEF TONGUE WITH SPINACH

PRIME RIBS OF BEEF AU JUS

STEAMED POTATOES BUTTERED ASPARAGUS

* * * * * * * *

CHERRY PIE

* * * * *

AMERICAN, SWISS AND PIMIENTO CHEESE

COFFEE TEA POSTUM CHOCOLATE.

In 1937 the National Park Service using a government's Works Progress Administration grant begin the construction of the McKinley Park Hotel, about 300 yards west of the train station. The next year it was turned over to the railroad and opened for the 1939 summer season. The hotel could accommodate up to 200 overnight guests. It had a large lobby, dining room, cocktail lounge, snack bar, facilities for programs, an employee dormitory, and a power plant. During World War II, the US Army took it over as a rest and relaxation center for troops in Alaska. Again, during the Korean War, the Army and then the Air Force managed the hotel for their personnel. By 1953, the railroad took over the hotel again and it was opened only in the summer season. High demand for tourism hotel rooms led to a 48-room expansion. In 1972 a fire destroyed the 84-room main section and the expansion sustained heavy smoke and water damage. A new hotel was built using surviving structures, several old sleeping cars from the railroad and some new modular units. After the 2001 summer season the remaining hotel structures were removed. An ice-skating rink and a ski rope tow were added through the years.

A view of the hotel during World War II. —Anchorage Museum, Alaska Railroad Collection BL 79.2.4037

DENALI NATIONAL PARK AND PRESERVE

The park was established on February 19, 1917, with boundary extensions in 1922, 1932, and 1947. The original name of the park was Mount McKinley National Park after President William McKinley, who was elected in 1897. In 1980, the park's name was changed to Denali National Park & Preserve. The peak at 20,310 feet (Mount McKinley) was changed in 2015 to Denali. The 92-mile Park Road was completed in 1938 after 17 years of construction. Denali means "The High One" in native language. The Denali Highway was completed in 1957, giving access to the park and greatly expanding visitation. In 1971, the George Parks Highway was completed along the eastern end of the park. Many lodges and campgrounds have been built to give tourists a selection of places to stay while visiting the park.

Just north of the park entrance at Healy on the Parks Highway is the Usibelli Coal Mine, a family-owned-and-operated coal mine and the only operating coal mine in the state. Founded in 1943, the mine supplies ultra-low Sulphur coal to six interior Alaska power plants. In addition, from 1984–2016, it exported coal to Pacific Rim countries. As part of the mine's environmental steward goals, Usibelli pioneered a successful reclamation program six years before it was required by the state or federal law. The mine uses innovative and modern mining technologies. The "Ace-In-The-Hole" dragline is Alaska's largest land mobile machine, efficiently moving large volumes of dirt in the mining and reclamation processes. The company has over 80 years of reserves in its permitted mining areas. Today only guided tour groups are allowed to view the operation.

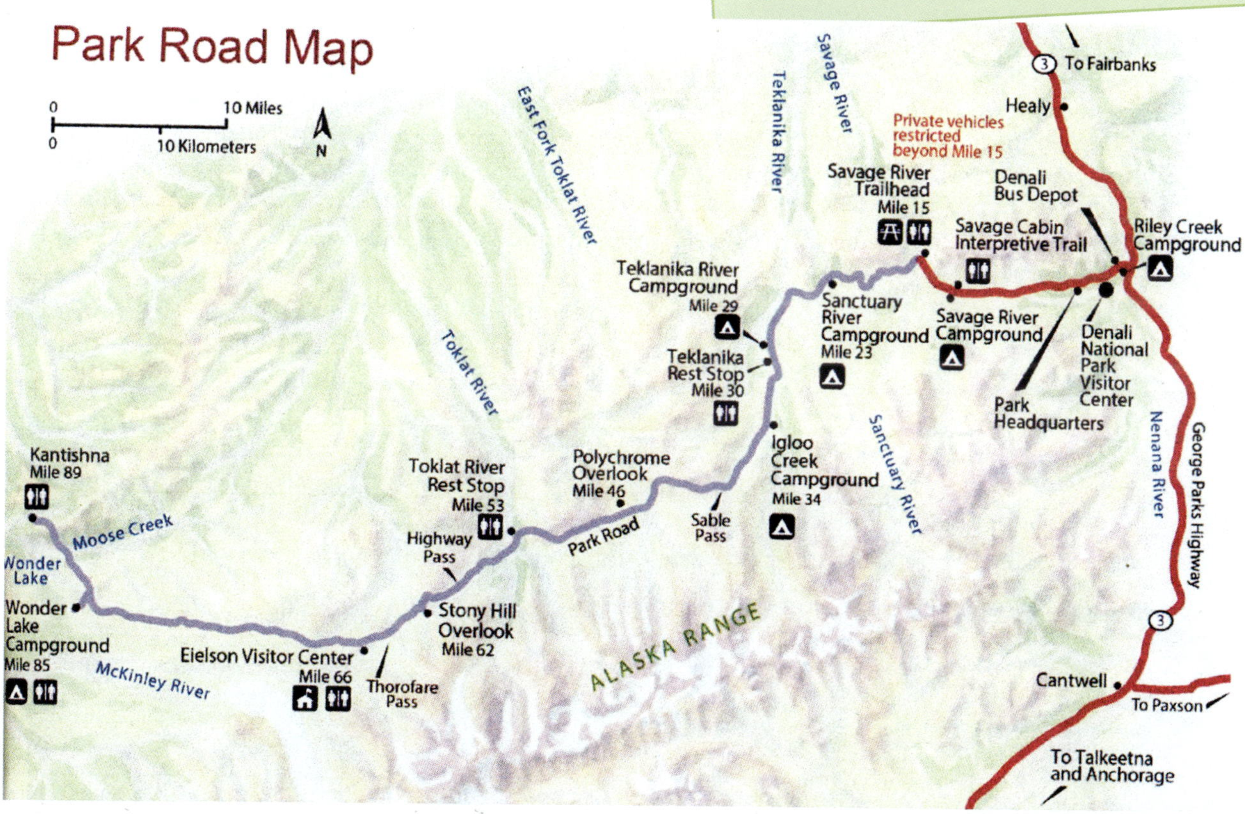

The Denali Park Road is 92 miles, running from east to west. Locations on the road are usually referred to by their mile number, meaning how many miles they are from the eastern end (the park entrance, Mile 0). The meeting of the Denali Park Road and Highway 3 (i.e., the park entrance) sits 237 miles north of Anchorage and 120 miles south of Fairbanks.
—National Park Service

THE COPPER RIVER AND NORTHWESTERN RAILWAY

The railway consisted of two rail lines, the Copper River line and the Northwestern line. A right-of-way was secured in 1904 up the Copper River and in 1906 rail construction started from Cordova, Alaska, north to the Kennecott copper ore mine owned by the Kennecott Corporation, which was part of the Alaska Syndicate, a group of very wealthy corporations invested in mining activity. A bridge named the "Million Dollar Bridge," finished in 1910, had to span the Kuskulana River Canyon and the Copper River. Copper ore first shipped in 1911 but in 1938 the ore finally ran out and the last ore train to Cordova ran on November 11. In the 1930s, the railway had 13 steam locomotives, six passenger cars, and 327 freight cars. The mining company donated the railroad right-of-way to the federal government for use as a public highway in 1941. A conversion of the bridge to vehicle traffic was started in 1953 and the bridge and the mining town of McCarthy are today major tourist attractions. The 60-mile McCarthy Road from the small mining town of Chitina ends on the Kennecott River, 0.5 mile before McCarthy and five miles from the historic Kennecott Mine, but the road needs to be driven with caution. There is lodging at McCarthy and Kennecott. —ASL Skinner Foundation Collection PCA 44-2-160

THE WHITE PASS & YUKON ROUTE

"Gold," the magic word that has caused thousands of people through the ages to pull up their roots and go off to seek fortunes, was flashed around the world in the summer of 1897 from news from The Klondike—or Klondyke. Many who headed to the last great gold strike in North America did not know the correct spelling, or even where it was in the vast continent. Most thought the gold fields were in Alaska, when actually they were in the Yukon in Canada.

This Gold Rush spawned a narrow-gauge railroad that would play an important part in the development of Alaska and northwestern Canada. But before the railroad was even a thought in anyone's mind, thousands of stampeders had headed north for the gold fields. The Klondike lay 650 miles north of the head of navigation at Skagway, at the end of the Lynn Canal and Dyea, Alaska. Other routes were a long trip up the Yukon River to the new town of Dawson City, a few miles from the rich gold fields, or a difficult trip through the Northwest Territories, and a few other very hazardous overland routes through Alaska and Canada, including the Dalton Trail.

Although the gold fields were in remote Canada, most of the stampeders were American or from distant countries. The gold had actually been discovered in 1896 but it took almost a year to get the word out and when it did it caused the greatest mass exodus in North American history, with perhaps 100,000 people starting on the trip but maybe half finishing. Dawson City was the melting pot for 30,000 and the largest city west of Winnipeg and north of Vancouver.

The two trails out of Skagway (Chilkoot) and Dyea (White), 10 miles away, were steep, difficult and dangerous. Pack animals could be used on the White Pass, but took a big toll on the animals, while the Chilkoot Pass was steeper and had to be walked carrying all a person's gear to last a year in the Canadian wilderness. A faster, less difficult and safer way had to be found to cross these passes.

A wagon road was built a short way on the White Pass Trail but soon a group of men looked at building a railroad across the pass. Most thought it was not feasible, except for one, Michael J. Henry, a former Canadian railroad contractor who thought it might work using a three-foot narrow-gauge track. Finances were obtained and construction began in April 1898 for a 110-mile route from Skagway to Whitehorse in the Yukon. The rails reached the summit on February 28, 1899 and Lake Bennett in British Columbia on July 6, 1899. In just 20 miles from its start, the roadbed rose from sea level to 3,000 feet. With construction starting at both ends they finally met at Carcross, Yukon, on July 29, 1900.

It was a historic construction project and through the next eight decades, including hauling

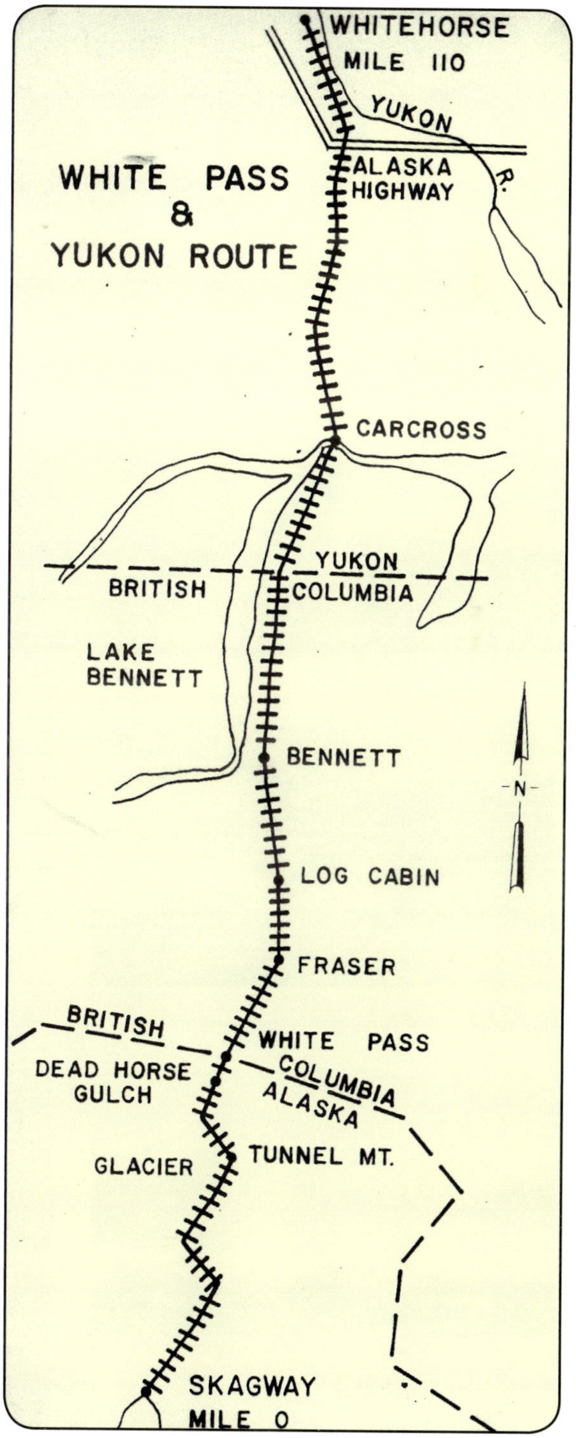

supplies for the military during World War II, it became the year-round gateway to the north. Ore from the Yukon mines and timber were hauled south to waiting ships at Skagway and passengers could go both ways for business or pleasure. When ore prices plummeted in 1982, the railroad was forced to suspend operations. By this time, air and land transportation were good alternatives for travel north. For years, however, the railroad also operated sternwheelers on the Yukon River and inland lakes and even started an air service.

In 1988 the White Pass reinvented itself as a strictly tourist railroad and today, in season one can take a trip to the summit, or on to Lake Bennett or finally to Carcross. The 1910 Bennett station is now a museum and lunch is served on the Bennett to Carcross section of the trip. The passenger cars have been redone to provide tables. This is a favorite excursion for passengers embarking at Skagway from the cruise boats.

Atlin is a small community located on the eastern shore of Atlin Lake in northwestern British Columbia and has been the scene of gold mining since 1898. The town has been a great tourist destination for years, first only accessible by river steamer until the Atlin Road was built in 1950–51. Surrounded by beautiful mountains it has been called the "Switzerland of the North," and is noted for hiking, fishing, and heliskiing with a milder winter climate than other parts of the region. The present-day, three-story Atlin Mountain Inn dates from the 1950s and provides comfortable accommodations.

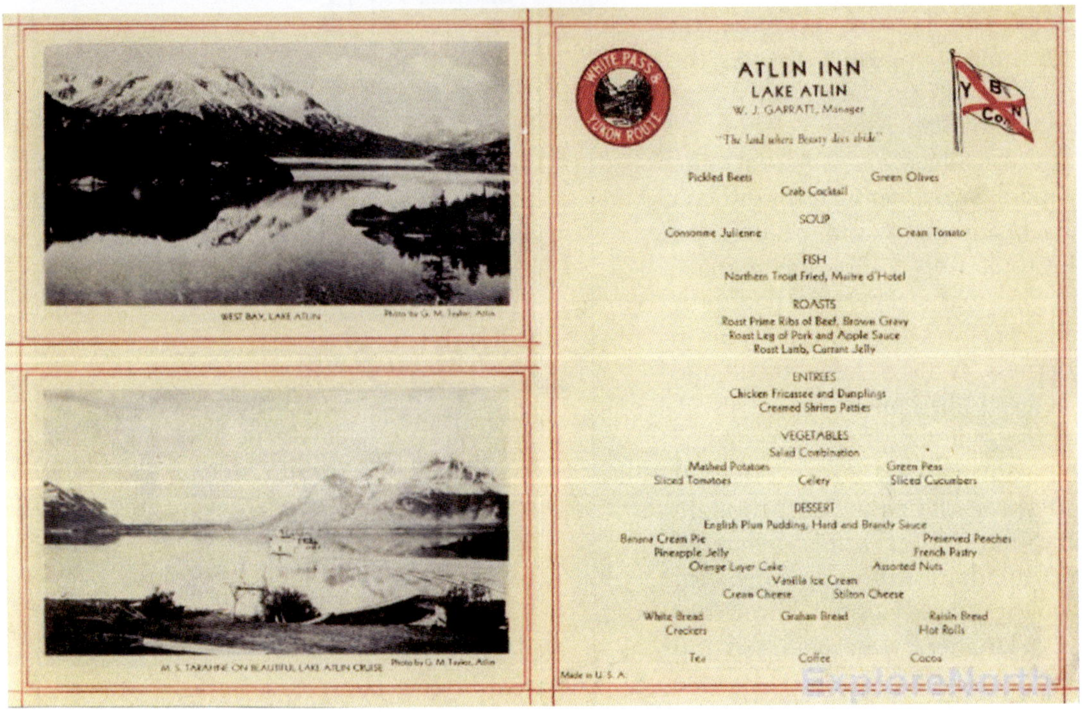

ATLIN INN
LAKE ATLIN
W. J. GARRATT, Manager

Pickled Beets — Green Olives
Crab Cocktail

SOUP
Consomme Julienne — Cream Tomato

FISH
Northern Trout Fried, Maitre d'Hotel

ROASTS
Roast Prime Ribs of Beef, Brown Gravy
Roast Leg of Pork and Apple Sauce
Roast Lamb, Currant Jelly

ENTREES
Chicken Fricassee and Dumplings
Creamed Shrimp Patties

VEGETABLES
Salad Combination
Mashed Potatoes — Green Peas
Sliced Tomatoes — Celery — Sliced Cucumbers

DESSERT
English Plum Pudding, Hard and Brandy Sauce
Banana Cream Pie — Preserved Peaches
Pineapple Jelly — French Pastry
Orange Layer Cake — Assorted Nuts
Vanilla Ice Cream
Cream Cheese — Stilton Cheese

White Bread — Graham Bread — Raisin Bread
Crackers — Hot Rolls

Tea — Coffee — Cocoa

Made in U. S. A.

A 1920s menu from the original inn, built by the railroad in 1916 to service the rise in tourism.

THE WHITE PASS & YUKON ROUTE

TRAFFIC DEPARTMENT

OFFICE OF GENERAL AGENT

HERMAN WEIG, GENERAL AGENT
1016 CHAMBER OF COMMERCE BUILDING
CHICAGO

IN YOUR REPLY PLEASE
REFER TO FILE

May 5,1905.

Mr. Albert H. Griffith,
Fisk, Wis.

Dear Sir:-

Referring to my letter to you regarding excursion rates to Dawson and Atlin: I shall consider it a great favor if you will kindly advise me whether you expect to take a trip to either of these places this coming summer.

It is expected the first "all expenses included" excursion to Atlin will take place from Seattle or Vancouver between June 25 and July 5. If you desire to take advantage of this excursion, particulars of which you have already received, it will be necessary for you to let me know as soon as possible as these Atlin excursion parties will be limited to 25 people each. If you cannot find it convenient to leave about the time mentioned above kindly advise me what date would suit you best. The exact date of the first excursion will be announced very soon.

I desire to impress upon you the fact that you will find the ocean steamers with which we connect running from Seattle and Vancouver to Skaguay are first class in every respect, affording passengers every comfort and convenience. Those for whom we make reservations will be given the very best selections at no additional expense, provided of course application is made in sufficient time.

In respect to the service on our river steamers; what is stated our booklet is borne out by the following by Mr. J. S. McLain in his in book on Alaska and the Klondike which has just been published: "These boats are equal to any on the upper Mississippi, furnish comfortable accomodations, serve excellent meals and rob travel on the Yukon and its tributaries of every anticipated hardship."

Don't, however, overlook the fact that unless you go beyond the summit of White Pass you have only seen the shores of Alaska and to go as far as Skaguay without going "inside", as the residents of the interior put it, would be like going to France without seeing Paris; and really the interior of this wonderful Northland is more than worth a visit.

You will appreciate that it will be necessary for us to know about how many tourists there are to be taken care of this coming summer so that everything possible may be done for their comfort and with that end in view I shall, as stated above, be greatly obliged if you will advise me of your intentions. Should there be any further information that you desire won't you please write to me and I will be glad to answer your questions as fully as possible.

Yours faithfully,

Herman Weig, F.C.O.
General Agt.

The steel arched bridge spanning Dead Horse Gulch on the White Pass Trail was built in 1901 and was the highest steel cantilever bridge in the world at the time. Hundreds of pack animals lay dead in the gulch on the White Pass Trail during the height of the gold rush, abandoned by their drivers as conditions were too harsh for these animals. —AC

The last steam engine was retired from service in 1964, but engine #73, which was displayed at Bennett for years, has been restored and been used for short excursions, bringing back memories of the early days of railroading. The railroad can lay claim to having the northernmost operating steam locomotive on the continent. —AC

White Pass and Yukon Route

At Skagway begins the White Pass and Yukon Railway which conquers the "almost impossible" on its way toward Dawson and the Klondike. Scenic features include Denver Glacier, Pitchfork Falls, Bridal Veil Falls, White Pass City, Glacier Gorge, Sawtooth Mountains, Lake Bennett and White Horse Rapids. Train trip to Lake Bennett can be made while your ship docks, $7.50. Luncheon at Bennett $1.00.

NORTHBOUND			Distance from Skagway	Altitude in Feet	W. P. and Y. Schedules:—	SOUTHBOUND		
No. 5	No. 3	No. 1				No. 2	No. 4	No. 6
Sunday Wednesday Friday	Monday Tuesday Thursday Saturday	Sunday Wednesday Friday				Sunday Wednesday Friday	Monday Tuesday Thursday Saturday	Monday Thursday Saturday
*‡8:30 am	*8:30 am	*10:00 am	0.0	0	Lv. . . Skagway . . Ar.	4:30 pm	4:30 pm	3:00 pm
. . . . . .	11:30 am	1:00 pm	. . . . .	. . . . .	Ar. c. Bennett Lv.	1:55 pm	1:40 pm	12:26 pm
10:40 am	12:01 pm	1:30 pm	40.6	2,158	Lv. c. Bennett Ar.	1:30 pm	1:15 pm	12:01 pm
11:59 am	1:30 pm	3:00 pm	. . . . .	. . . . .	Ar. Carcross Lv.	12:10 pm	12:15 pm	10:45 am
1:00 pm	1:40 pm	3:05 pm	67.5	2,164	Lv. Carcross Ar.	11:40 am	11:50 am	10:35 am
3:00 pm	3:50 pm	5:05 pm	110.7	2,079	Ar. White Horse . Lv.	9:30 am	9:30 am	8:45 am

*‡Alaska Time—One hour behind Pacific Time. c Meal Station.
‡West Taku Arm Special, leaves from Skagway Wharf—Other trains leave from Skagway Depot.

A 32-hour trip can be taken on the White Pass & Yukon to West Taku Arm of Lake Tagish. A special train leaves the Skagway wharf for Carcross, where the steamer "Tutshi" is boarded for the trip up the narrow mountain lakes to Ben-My-Chree, at the head of West Taku Arm, and to Taku Glacier. The cost of this trip is $35.00, not including parlor car fare.

Tourists viewing the St. Andrews Presbyterian Church on the shore of Lake Bennett in British Columbia. Built in 1898, it is the only remaining building from the gold rush days. A cemetery is just above the church. Bennett was the end of both the White Pass and Chilkoot trails, and from here, stampeders had to build boats for a 400+ mile trip by water on the Yukon River, to Dawson City. The church is still intact for trail hikers to visit. The 1910 train station is a designated Heritage Railway Station Museum. —ASL Skinner Collection PCA 44-2-210

CARIBOU HOTEL AND MATTHEW WATSON GENERAL STORE

The Caribou Hotel, a Yukon Historic Site, was originally built in Bennett in 1898 and was named the Yukon Hotel. After the gold rush was over, it was floated down Lake Bennett to the present Carcross site and renamed the Anderson Hotel. In 1903, Dawson Charlie, co-discoverer of the Klondike Gold Strike, bought the hotel and operated it until his death in 1908. Edwin and Bessie Gideon continued to run it until it burned down and a new building rose from the ashes in 1910. Bessie died in 1933 and her ghost has supposedly haunted the hotel ever since. The hotel was purchased by Anne Morgan and Jamie Toole in 2006 and refurbished, and is one of the Yukon's longest continuously operating food and beverage establishments. Its most famous guest was "Polly the Parrot" who resided there from 1918 to 1972 and was very talkative.

The Matthew Watson General Store in Carcross, next to the Caribou Hotel, brings back visions of the gold rush of 1898 with its many antique fixtures and original goods sold at the time. It is open summers only and has a selection of gold rush souvenirs and a great ice cream parlor.

A major stop on the railroad or by vehicle is Carcross, Yukon, on the shores of Bennett and Nares lakes. It is the home of the Carcross/Tagish First Nation. The village, originally named Caribou Crossing, was the scene of the Golden Spike Ceremony for the railroad on July 29, 1900, linking Skagway with Whitehorse. The sternwheeler Tutshi and its visitors' center were major attractions in town until they burned down in 1990. Other attractions include the fastest freighter in the Yukon, (MV Sibilla), the Carcross Desert, Caribou Crossing Trading Post, Bennett Beach, Carcross Commons Artisans that include a themed playground, boutiques, food, totem pole carvings, and a Vistor Information Center, the railroad station and museum, and the town itself, with many antique buildings. Mountain biking and hiking trails are available.

An early view of the Carcross train depot. Notice the Railway Express Agency sign on the building. The depot has been upgraded through the years and is now a museum. —AC

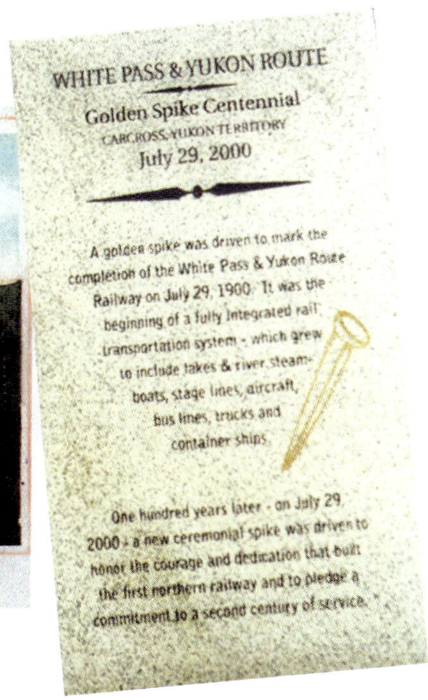

White Pass

GOLD RUSH ADVENTURE

STRIKE IT RICH in history, scenery and fun along the White Pass Railway **highway-link** between Skagway and Whitehorse.

All the color and romance of the Klondike Gold Rush is yours to enjoy. You can see it in the decor of your comfortable railway 'view-coach' . . . in the mysterious depths of Dead Horse Gulch . . . the thrilling view of White Pass Summit, and the original Klondike Trail of '98 which runs right beside the track.

You will follow the trail of the sourdoughs through the most inspiring scenery in North America. Roaring rivers and quiet emerald lakes combine with the majestic St. Elias mountains to create a breathtaking panorama of natural beauty.

If you are motoring, take your car with you **on the same train.** Take advantage of the economical 'Package Plan.' Man and wife and car (either way—Skagway to Whitehorse or Whitehorse to Skagway) for $79.00. Additional members of the family travel at reduced rates.

For Skagway stop-over travelers there is a special 'Day On The Trail of '98' tour between Skagway and Lake Bennett. Luncheon snack is served to all White Pass travelers at historic Bennett—where the sourdoughs built their boats and rafts on their journey to the Klondike.

Spend a Day on the Trail or Make your Highway Link the White Pass. It's the trip of a lifetime.

"THERE'S FUN FOR THE WHOLE FAMILY IN THE GLITTERING NORTH"

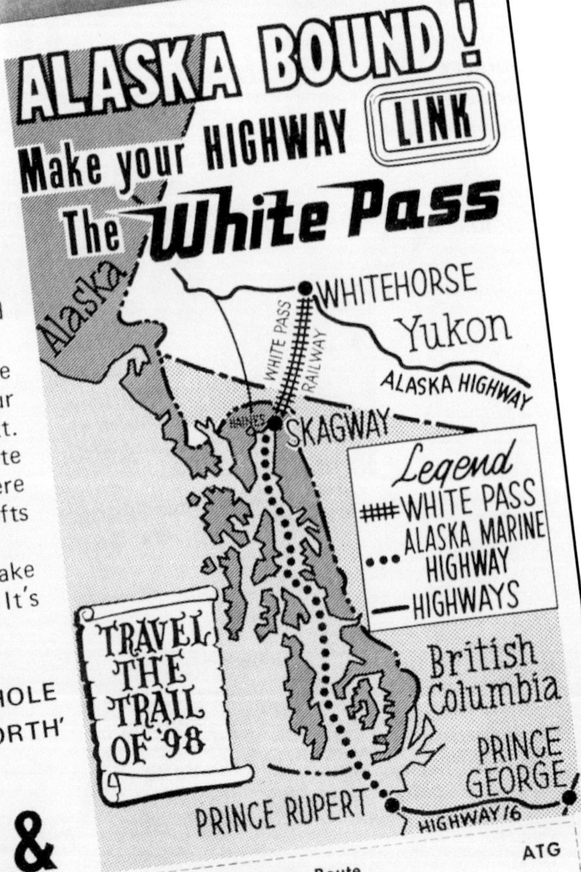

WHITE PASS & YUKON ROUTE

FRANK G. DOWNEY
Passenger Traffic Manager
1226 Vance Building, P. O. Box 2147
Seattle, Washington 98111

ATG

White Pass & Yukon Route
P. O. Box 2147
Seattle, Washington 98111
Please send information and folder on Alaska Yukon tours.

Name..
Address.............................. State.............
City..

The Administration Building and annex in Skagway were constructed in 1900 and donated to the National Park Service in 1976 for use as office space and museum. In 1998, The Klondike Gold Rush National Historical Park joined with Chilkoot Trail National Historic Site, Dawson Historical Complex National Historic Site, and "The Thirty Mile" stretch of the Yukon River to form Klondike Gold Rush International Historical Park. —Yukon Archives, Whitehorse

The White Pass & Yukon Route depot waiting room and gift shop. —NPS David Curl Photo

The stately railroad administration building and depot has been restored and is now the home of the National Park Service's offices and visitor's center.
—NPS David Curl Photo

Diesel locomotive #93, built in 1956, pulling some cars on the back side of the Administration building. The railroad started converting to diesel locomotives in 1954. —AC

TOWNS AND CITIES IN ALASKA/YUKON

JUNEAU

This area was first explored and surveyed in 1794 by the English navigator Vancouver. Placer gold was discovered in 1869, 60 miles from Juneau. Two prospectors, Richard Harris and Joe Juneau, found a great quantity of gold in 1880 in the area and then discovered a rich gold quartz deposit in what was known as Silver Bow Basin. With this strike, a smaller but similar rush like the later Klondike gold rush began. The 160-acre platted boom town was named a townsite in 1880 and first called Harrisburg, then Rockwell, and finally Juneau in the Gastineau Channel.

The Treadwell Mine, on Douglas Island, just off shore of Juneau was another large discovery and mined for 36 years until 1917, when it caved in. The transfer of the capital of the territory from Sitka was completed by 1906, and by 1930 the present capitol building was opened. The three main mining operations through the years were the Treadwell, the Alaska-Juneau, and the Alaska-Gastineau.

Today, Juneau is a busy town with state and federal offices and a major tourist stop for cruise boats, private boats and aircraft, the Alaska Marine Highway, and airlines. Places to visit include South Franklin Street with its antique buildings, the State Capitol and Governor's mansion, The Alaska State Museum and the Juneau-Douglas Museum, The Sealaska Heritage Institute, Mendenhall Glacier, Mount Roberts Tramway, Saint Nicholas Russian Orthodox Church, the Last Chance Mining District, the Red Dog Saloon, the Alaskan Hotel, and flightseeing tours of the Juneau Ice Cap and Glacier Bay National Park and Preserve. Also, hiking and skiing are available. On July 1, 1970, Juneau merged with the city of Douglas for a combined borough.

A postcard view of the extensive Alaska-Juneau mining complex where today tours are offered. Juneau is situated in what is known as the "Juneau Gold Belt." Placer gold was first discovered in the district in the early 1880s in Gold Creek. Later discoveries of quartz gold deposits were found in the hills back of Juneau. A number of mining operations soon followed, including this large one.

Historic Franklin Street with its antique buildings from the gold rush days and gift shops lining the street.
—AC

GLACIER HIGHWAY

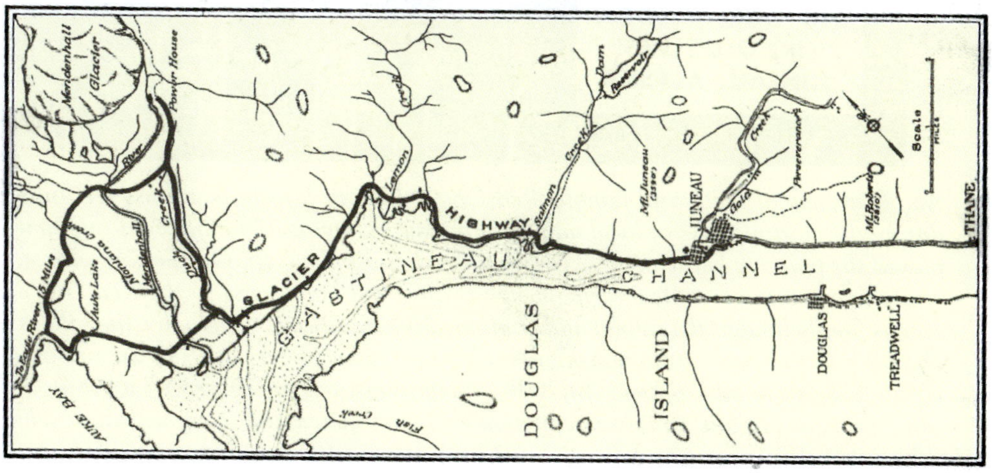

The Glacier Highway is 13 miles long.

A view of the Baranof Hotel, Juneau's finest, was built in 1939 in Art Deco fashion. In 1979, floors 7, 8, and 9 were added, totaling 215 rooms now and the outside façade was redone. —AC

An older view of the world-famous Red Dog Saloon in Juneau is a must-see tourist stop. It was first established during the glorious days of local mining with liquor, singing and dancing. Long time entertainer, "Ragtime Hattie" played the piano in her white gloves and silver dollar halter top. Gordie Kanouse, a 20-year owner would meet the cruise boats with his mule wearing a sign stating "follow my ass to the Red Dog Saloon." In the early 1970s the Harris family bought the saloon and continued the traditions. Originally, the saloon was located on Franklin Street and later moved next to the Alaskan Hotel on the same street. In 1988 the saloon was moved again to its present site at 278 So. Franklin Street. In 2008, the business was purchased by a group of local people and continues to offer a unique antique atmosphere, with a Red Dog Mercantile store next door selling souvenirs and apparel.

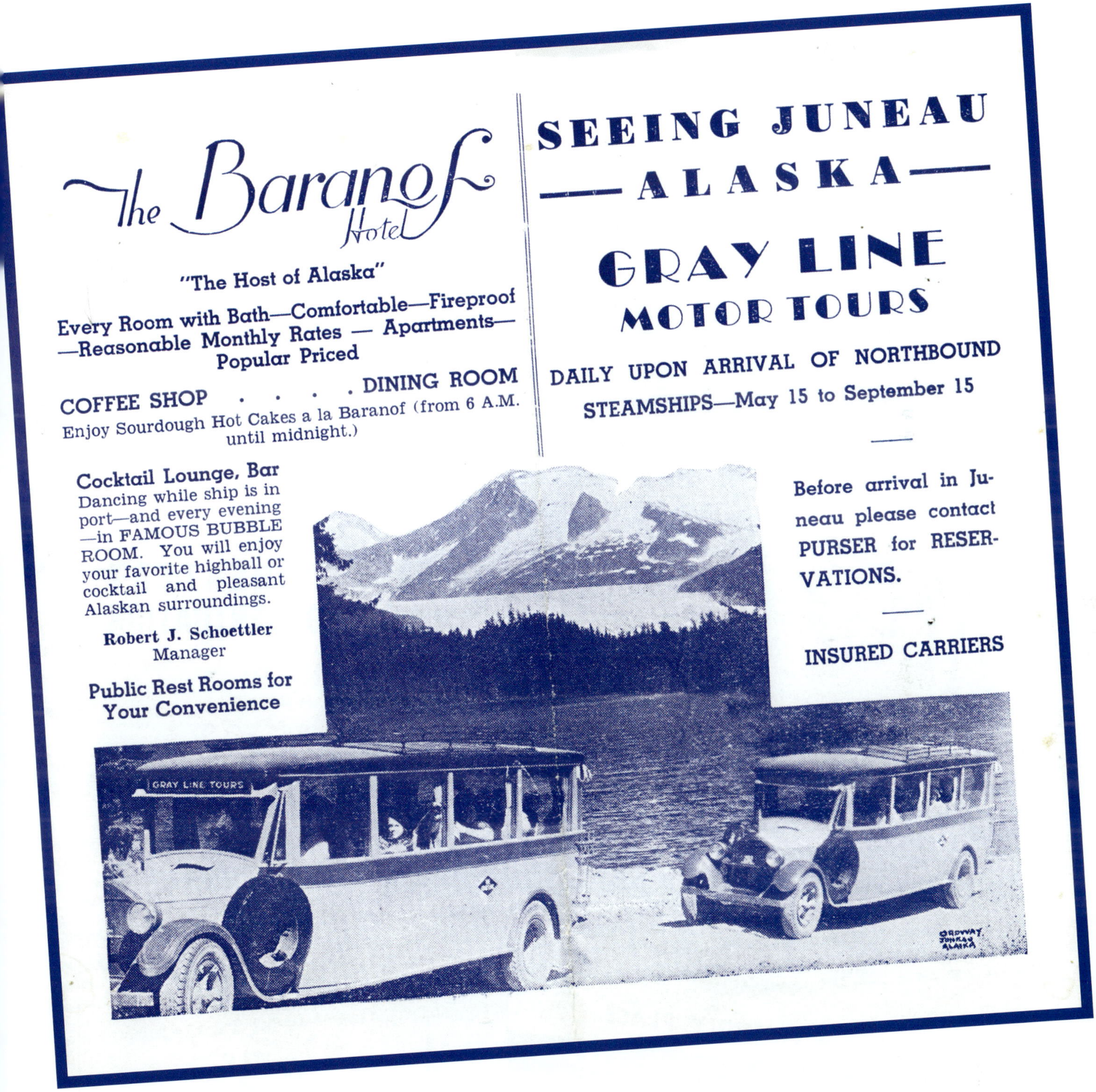
The Baranof Hotel
"The Host of Alaska"
Every Room with Bath—Comfortable—Fireproof —Reasonable Monthly Rates — Apartments— Popular Priced
COFFEE SHOP . . . . . DINING ROOM
Enjoy Sourdough Hot Cakes a la Baranof (from 6 A.M. until midnight.)
Cocktail Lounge, Bar
Dancing while ship is in port—and every evening —in FAMOUS BUBBLE ROOM. You will enjoy your favorite highball or cocktail and pleasant Alaskan surroundings.
Robert J. Schoettler
Manager
Public Rest Rooms for Your Convenience
SEEING JUNEAU
—ALASKA—
GRAY LINE
MOTOR TOURS
DAILY UPON ARRIVAL OF NORTHBOUND STEAMSHIPS—May 15 to September 15
Before arrival in Juneau please contact PURSER for RESERVATIONS.
INSURED CARRIERS
GRAY LINE TOURS
ORDWAY JUNEAU ALASKA

KETCHIKAN

Ketchikan is the seat of the Ketchikan Gateway Borough and became known as "Alaska's First City" It is at the southern tip of the Inside Passage. The Tlingit natives used Ketchikan Creek for years for a summer fish camp and the town was established in 1885 by Mike Martin and incorporated in 1900. The largest industry was the Ketchikan Pulp Company, which opened a mill on the shores of Ward Cove in 1964. It was closed in 1997. Canneries, a shipyard, and forestry, along with a large tourist trade have kept the economy stabilized. The city has the largest collection of standing totem poles in the world with displays at Saxman Park, Totem Bight State Park, Potlatch Park, and the Totem Heritage Park. Nearby is Misty Fiords National Monument which reminds one of the fiords of Scandinavia.

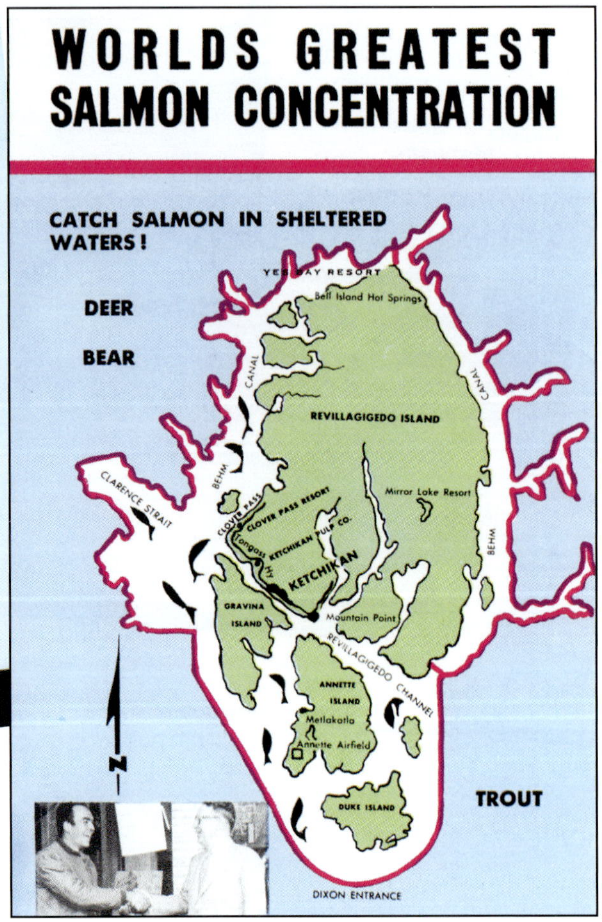

"New Town" Ketchikan, Alaska.

VIEW DOWN TONGASS NARROWS, KETCHIKAN, ALASKA
62755-C

WELCOME VISITORS
S-343 Mission Street - Ketchikan, Alaska from the Boat Deck
Schallerer ©

The Alaska Sportsman magazine was, for many years, Alaska's media outlet for the outside world. It catered to locals, hunters, fishermen and people who dreamed of making a trip to the North. Its office was in Ketchikan.

Indian Made Slate Totem Poles, Wood Totem Poles, Thlinket and Haida Baskets made from Spruce roots, Cedar bark. Also the famous Attu Baskets, the finest Baskets made. Genuine Chilkat Blankets, all kinds Eskimo Ivory Carvings and Curios.

All kinds of Alaska Nugget and old Ivory Jewelry, Nugget Chains, Bracelets, Pins, Charms, Knives, Brooches Belt Buckles, Indian Carved Bracelets, Spoons and Forks. Souvenir Spoons, Old Fossil Walrus Ivory Beads. Souvenirs and Post Cards.

PRUELL'S GIFT SHOP

Among the very interesting curios to be seen, is a chest that shows the joining of the wood by means of sewing. It is considered one of the special accomplishments of the Northwest Coast Indians. The construction may have been taken over from birchbark work of the sort done by the interior tribes; but if so, great skill is shown in the application of this process to woodwork. The threads of spruce root are often concealed in deep grooves, so as to be unnoticed unless sought for. We also have perhaps one of the oldest Tenna or Coppers in existence, being made from the native copper, found near the Copper River district. These Coppers were only owned by very rich Chiefs, and were prized more highly than anything else that they owned. This Copper of Tenna also shows the number of slaves owned by the family, by the marks on it. Among other interesting curios, hundreds of years old, are stone cooking utensils, old adzes used in making Canoes and Totems, old Fossil ivory sled runners used by the Eskimos, and various other bone, ivory, stone utensils and implements too numerous to mention, many of these curios are not for sale but it is always a pleasure to show them and explain their meaning.

OUR PRICES ARE THE SAME TO TOURISTS AS TO OUR LOCAL CUSTOMERS

BE SURE TO VISIT ALASKA'S FINEST CURIO SHOP

TOURISTS—You will find the Most Complete Collection of Curios in Alaska at—

Pruell's Gift Shop — New Ingersoll Hotel Building — Ketchikan, Alaska

DISTANCES FROM SEATTLE, WASHINGTON

	Miles
Seymour Narrows	209
Prince Rupert	572
KETCHIKAN	662
Wrangell	749
Petersburg	791
Juneau	899
Skagway	1000
Whitehorse	1111
Dawson	1584
Sitka	1060
Cordova	1400
Kennecott	1596
Valdez	1490
Latouche	1596
Seward	1700
Anchorage	1814
Nenana	2100
Fairbanks	2167
Nome	2621

YOU'RE IN SKAGWAY. WHAT WILL YOU DO?

When you come to our town, if you do not go right away again to take one of the beautiful RAILROAD trips, you will doubtless have some time to spare, and will wonder how to avoid aimless walking about; the kind that makes your legs ache and your interests lag. Well here are a few suggestions.

Take the TROLLFY-CAR ride with Martin Itjen, 50¢. Without this experience, no trip to Skagway is really complete, You will hear all about the history of Skagway, with many interesting personalties and details, including the tame fish. This takes from two to three hours, however, so if you are pressed for time, at least see Skagway, if not through the eyes of the romantic Mr. Itjen, with one of the other TAXI COMPANIES who also conduct sightseeing trips, at the same rates.

Another delightful way to see the town and also the surrounding country, is to take a short AIRPLANE ride, weather permitting. Nothing could well equal this in grandeur of natural beauty.

You will not want to leave town without visiting the various CURIO SHOPS, PHOTO SHOPS, and the ART SHOP, in which you may see many of the paintings of Mr.

SKAGWAY

Situated at the head of Lynn Canal is the site of much importance to the history of the Klondike Gold Rush. The town of Skagway or Skaguay was the start of the White Pass trail and Dyea, 10 miles from Skagway, at the mouth of the Taiya River was the start of the Chilkoot Trail. Dyea is gone now but the site has been developed by Alaska X with tourist attractions. Skagway is a true tourist town with many original buildings from the Gold Rush days, the starting point for the scenic White Pass & Yukon Route, the Skagway Museum, the Corrington's Alaskan Ivory Museum, guided walking and antique bus tours of the area, the Red Onion Brothel Saloon, Lairsville Gold Rush Trail Camp and salmon bake, Mollie Walsh Park, Captain William Moore Cabin, the Gold Rush Cemetery, and many gift and souvenir shops. The town was platted in the late 1890s by Captain William Moore, but with thousands of stampeders reaching the town on their way north, Moore was pushed off his land and the town became a "wild frontier" settlement. But by 1910, with other gold rush areas in Alaska drawing off new stampeders (Nome and Fairbanks), Skagway was stabilized with the railroad as its main business and employment.

The US Courthouse just off Broadway was constructed in 1899 by the Methodist Church. It was Alaska's first granite structure and soon housed McCabe College, Alaska's first institution of higher learning. The district court was dissolved in the 1950s and the building was later added to. Today, it houses city hall and the Trail of '98 Museum. —AC

FRYE-BRUHN CO.

Packers and Jobbers of

Fresh Meats

Poultry and Provisions

Fish and Game
In Season

Special Attention Given to Mail Orders

P. O. Box 246

SKAGWAY, ALASKA

Skagway
Alaska

THE ONLY GATEWAY TO THE INTERIOR OF ALASKA AND THE YUKON

THE IDEAL PLACE TO BUILD A HOME
PLENTY OF ROOM FOR ALL

Compiled by
PHIL ABRAHAMS
Established 1897
For Information Write

Skagway An Outfitting Center

Skagway is the supply point for the miner, prospector and the homeseeker. The merchants carry large stocks of goods in every line, and it has been demonstrated to those who have outfitted in the States, that after paying freight and other charges to have their outfits landed at the Skagway wharf from the ship, that they could have saved in good hard cash not less than twenty-five per cent. Anything that can be purchased in the lower coast cities can be bought here, and for less money. You can buy groceries, hardware, clothing, boots, shoes, fur robes, drugs, and everything that is necessary for an interior trip, to much better advantage, and the merchant here can tell you what you ought to have, and what you ought not to have, much better than those who have not had the Alaska business experience in outfitting.

The White Pass Railway

Will take you over to any point so that you may make connections for the Atlin gold mining camp, Whitehorse, Dawson, and any point on the Yukon river. And by coming to Skagway you will find that this is the only real gateway to the interior of Alaska.

Mining

To the prospector, there is ample opportuniry for him at and near Skagway; there are good openings, and somewhere nearby the lucky man will strike it rich. So far the mountains have hardly been scratched, and that the mineral is there, there is no doubt.

In 1923, the Princess Steamship Company began to call at Skagway. The local people wanted to put on a show for the tourists that told the history of Skagway and its unique characters, especially Soapy Smith. "Days of 98" is still in operation and presents four shows a day during the tourist season. The show runs just under an hour and the evening show has 30 minutes of a mock casino and gambling for the customers. —AC

The Fraternal Order of Eagles purchased the Pacific Hotel in 1902 and it underwent a major remodel in 1916–17. It was moved it to its present location around 1920, and was attached to the rear of the Mondamin building and the "Days of 98" theater show has used the site for years. —AC

P. E. Kern's *jewelry store served as a backdrop for this photo of a collection of 250-pound mastodon tusks, excavated from the Hunker Creek area of the Klondike in 1905. Kern was one of several prominent jewelers in Skagway in the early part of the century.* —University of Alaska, J.B. Moore Collection archives

The Arctic Brotherhood Hall was built in the summer of 1899 with the driftwood and stick façade added a year later. The steamship building was built in 1900. The hall is owned by the city, and housed city hall from 1938–46. It has also been an art shop, museum, and visitor center. —AC

Broadway in the 1930s with the tracks running down the middle of the street. They were laid down in 1898 and were not taken up until the end of World War II. The Dewey Hotel, now gone, is on the right. Richter's store has been in business for many years. —AC

ALASKAX

Alaska X is a locally owned and operated company with a focus on providing affordable and immersive tour experiences in the remote wilderness. Its Eco conscious tours will leave one with not only extraordinary memories, but a greater appreciation and understanding of Alaskan nature and heritage. This all started in 1991 and in 1994 a facility was established at the old historic townsite of Dyea, about 10 miles from Skagway. Dyea was the starting point for the Klondike stampeders on their 36-mile hike, climbing over the steep Chilkoot Pass to Lake Bennett. Skagway was the other starting point for the rugged White Pass Trail, now crossed by the narrow-guage White Pass & Yukon Route. At Dyea a maze of zip lines and suspension or swinging bridges have been installed to give the visitor a wild ride through the wilderness. The 1994 facility, Adventure Camp, was opened and since that time other camps were added, including Musher's Camp and S'mores Roasting and Musher's Camp and Gold Panning. Alaska X also has a canoe tour to the Davidson Glacier, called Glacier Point Wilderness Safaris, which is located about 15 miles south of Skagway. The trip from Skagway to Dyea to get to the Adventure Camp is narrated, and includes the Slide Cemetery where in 1898, 65 people were killed in an avalanche.

Herman Krimse came north in 1897 and opened Skagway's first jewelry and watch repair store in a tent. In 1906, he moved into the present building and had totem poles carved next to the store. He worked with gold and reportedly made the largest and smallest gold nugget chains in the world. A jewelry store is still there and has displayed many historical artifacts. —AC

Golden North Hotel
SKAGWAY, ALASKA
"Cleanest In The North"
60 Rooms—20 With Bath
TEAM HEAT
James Tropea, Proprietor

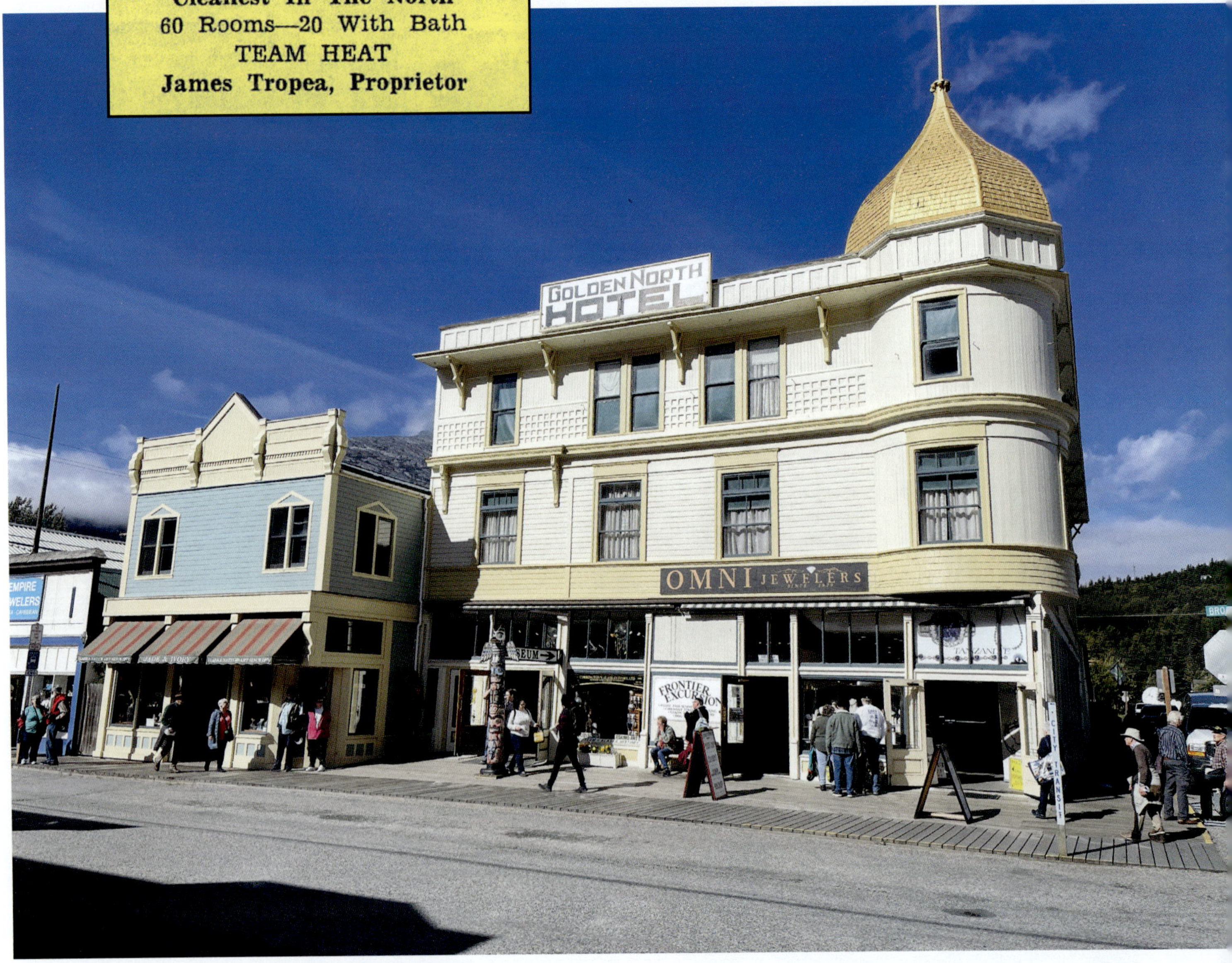

The Klondike Trading Company built a two-story structure in 1898 on the corner of Third and State. In 1908, the structure was moved to its present location on Broadway, a third story was added, and it was reopened as the Golden North Hotel. The building went through some financial difficulties through the years with many different uses; mainly as a hotel and a bar and restaurant. It is now owned by long-time Skagway business people Corrington's Enterprises. It now houses Omni Jewelers, Frontier Excursions, two gift shops, and the very popular Corrington's Alaskan Ivory Museum. —Corrington's Enterprises photo

The Pullen House Hotel

As Skagway was at one time Alaska's largest city, it was only natural that it was the site of the largest and most elaborate hotel—the Pullen House. Established by Mrs. Harriet Pullen a few years after the gold rush, it remained one of the North's leading hotels through the first half of the century.

She arrived in Skagway in September 1897 with her husband, whom she later divorced. She established a tent restaurant, then a log building but eventually joined the rush to the Atlin gold strike.

Returning to Skagway she became one of the few women packers over the White Pass Trail. Her next project was a boarding house. She rented a large frame house from Capt. William Moore. She later purchased it and named it the Pullen House. She and it became very well-known and after spending 50 years running her elaborate hotel, the Grand Lady of the North died at 87 in 1947.

The hotel finally succumbed to economic difficulties in the 1950s. Weather and vandalism caused the building to be torn down, along with a later annex addition, and the site was cleaned up.

—AC

The Skagway Inn was built in 1897 and operated through the years as a brothel, a family residence, a boarding house, and now is a frontier country Inn as a Bed & Breakfast. —AC

The White House was originally a home built in the early 1900s. During the war the US Army took it over for use as a hospital. It is now a Bed and Breakfast. —AC

It takes an unusual person to go charging off into the wilderness in pursuit of gold. As one might suspect, gold rush towns—be they in California, South Dakota or on the banks of the Chena River in Fairbanks or the beaches of Nome, Alaska—contained their share of characters.

The Klondike Rush, perhaps more so than others, included many unusual and eccentric individuals whose deeds have been characterized in both fiction and nonfiction writings, plays and even movies. Skagway was home to a number of them.

Martin Itjen

In the decades after the gold rush, Martin Itjen was probably the city's most colorful resident. He came north from Florida in 1898 to join the stampede but only got as far as Atlin, British Columbia. He eventually made it to Skagway and spent the next 40 years running a rooming house, an undertaking business and Skagway's first Ford auto agency. His most famous venture however, was his Skagway Street Car Company.

This marvel of transportation was built on a Ford chassis and resembled a bus. The streetcars (eventually there were four) contained a remarkable collection of gadgetry and other peculiar items, including a stuffed bear and a life-sized mannequin of Soapy Smith, which would "perform" when Itjen worked a series of foot pedals. Itjen drove the streetcar up and down the streets of Skagway during the 1920s and '30s showing the tourists the sights of the town.

Never a man to let grass grow under his feet, Itjen purchased Soapy Smith's parlor in 1935 and converted it to a museum, eventually adding many Alaskan artifacts to its historical collections. The museum was later sold to some long-time Skagway residents and they moved the building and contents to Skagway's waterfront, where it was operated for many more years. After their deaths, the building was purchased by the Rasmuson Foundation and donated to the National Park Service in 2008. It has been restored and opened to the public.

Itjen was known for his sense of humor. On a trip to Hollywood in 1935, driving his streetcar, for example, he invited movie star Mae West to come to Skagway and serve as a hostess on his streetcars. Itjen died in 1942 and next to his grave is a large rock, painted gold. On it are the words "The biggest nugget in the world."

—AC

—AC

SOAPY SMITH

Jefferson Randolph "Soapy" Smith probably ranks as one of Skagway's best-known characters from the gold rush days. Certainly, he was its most notorious con man. It is said at the height of the gold rush, Smith and his gang virtually controlled the town, a reign that ended in a shoot-out with one of Skagway's leading citizens, Frank Reid.

Smith was born in Georgia in 1860 to parents who were both members of prominent Southern families. He spent his formative years in Texas, where his family moved in the 1870s. After several different jobs growing up, he discovered his gift for gab, which would keep him going until he showed up in Skagway. When still in his teens, Smith was hired on as a trail hand on cattle drives, and spent time drifting around the West. He eventually learned slight-of-hand tricks and made a living in the mining camps with gambling games such as the pea-under-the-shell game. He acquired his nickname "Soapy" from a game that involved hiding large bills in bars of soap.

Smith, who was generally opposed to violent methods, graduated to larger operations, and set up in Denver where he formed a gang. In Denver, he acquired a wide reputation for his con games as well as for his generosity to charities, churches and those in desperate need. He married a singer by the name of Anna Neilsen, whom he kept insulated from his "public" life and who eventually bore his children.

About 1890, Smith opened a gambling hall in Creede, Colorado, a wide-open mining town. After numerous run-ins with the law there and in Denver he left. He arrived in Skagway in August 1897, and opened his Jeff Smith's Parlor, which offered liquor and gambling. His intention was to take over the town with his gang. He set up a fake telegraph office to fleece the returning miners out of some of their hard-owned gold. He even set up a charity for adopting stray dogs. People generally liked him but had no use for his gang.

Some of the town leaders set up a vigilante-style "Committee of 101" to rid the town of the gang. Among the leaders was Frank Reid, a former Indian fighter and surveyor. The showdown between Smith and Reid began when a young miner arrived in Skagway from the Klondike carrying $2,700 in gold. Somehow, the miner and his gold were parted. The "Committee of 101" heard about this and, suspecting Smith and his gang, called a meeting on the Skagway wharf to take action. Smith tried to force his way into the meeting. On July 8, 1898 there was a struggle and Smith and Reid shot each other and both fell to the deck. Smith died immediately and Reid lingered for 12 days longer.

The gang scattered with some sent to prison. Reid and Smith were buried near each other at the Skagway cemetery. Reid's tombstone is imposing and Smith's has been was chipped away by souvenir hunters.

Jefferson Randolph "Soapy" Smith.
—Denver Public Library Collection

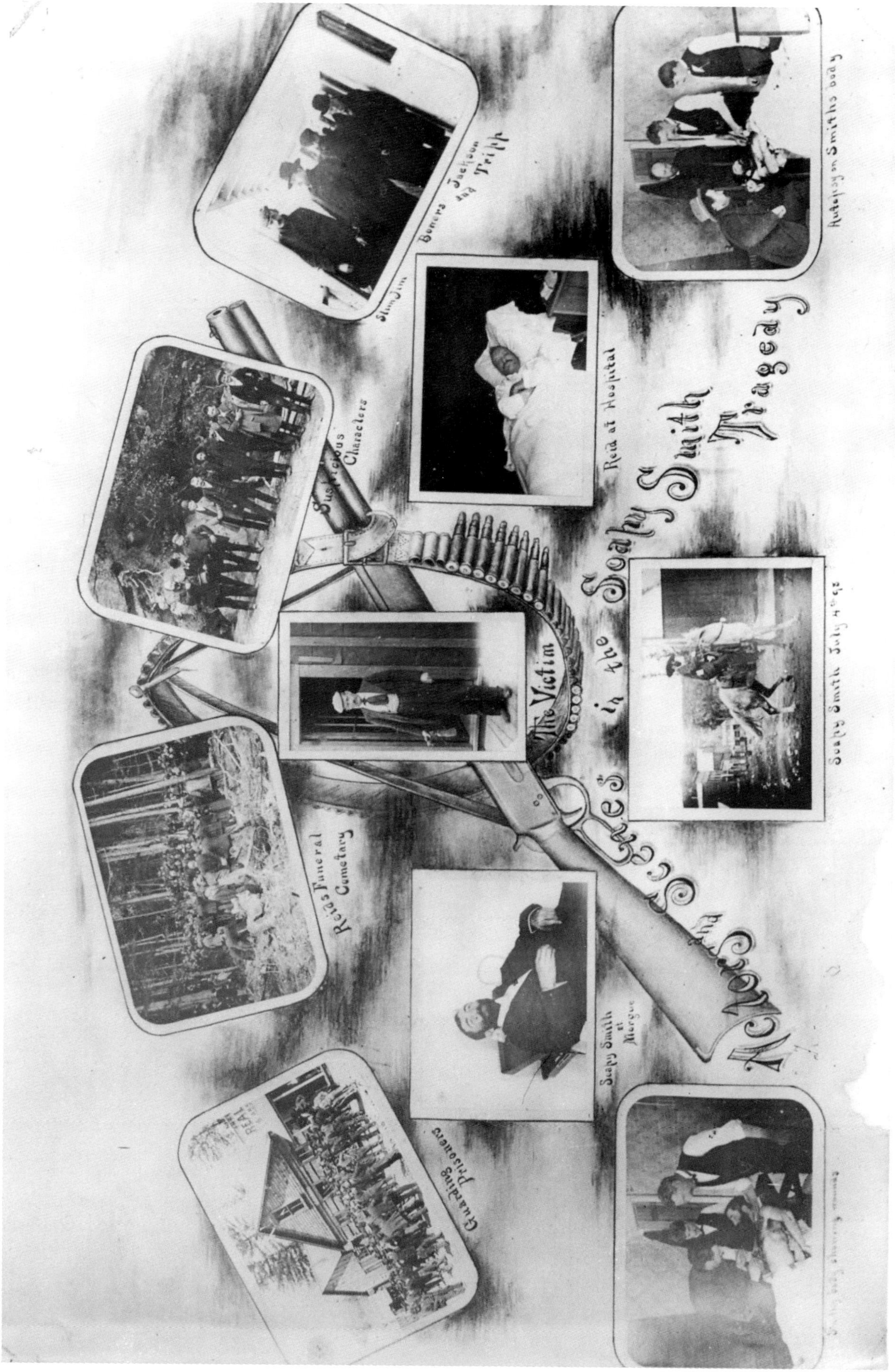
Scenes in the Soapy Smith Tragedy
Slim Jim Bowers Jackson and Tripp
Reid at Hospital
Autopsy on Smith's body
Suspicious Characters
The Victim
Soapy Smith July 4th 98
Reid's Funeral Cemetary
Soapy Smith at Morgue
Guarding Prisoners

THE KENAI PENINSULA

Our Point of View Lodge on Kenai Lake in 1963. It burned down years later.

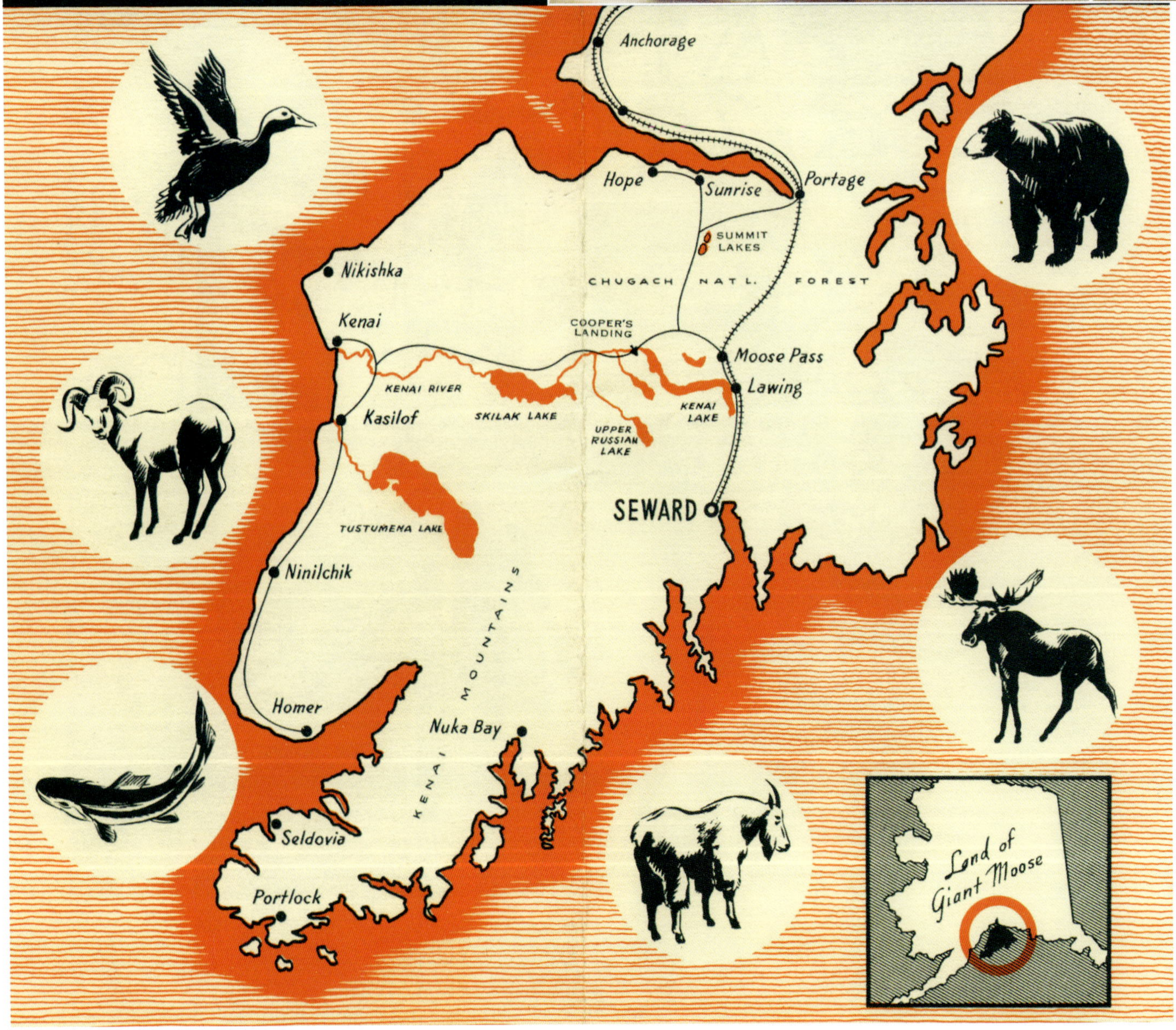

The Kenai Peninsula is a heavily visited area for sightseeing, boating, fishing, moose hunting, hiking, and gold panning on old placer gold deposits. It has a few small historic towns and large ones like Kenai, Homer, and Seward.

WRANGELL

Wrangell is the third oldest community in Alaska, founded by Russian traders in 1834. It is located at the mouth of the Stikine River, which is the largest river bisecting the Coast Mountains, and links Southeast Alaska with the interior. It is the only town in Alaska to have existed under three flags and four different nations. Three major gold rushes occurred up the river from 1861 to the 1890s. At one time it was as lawless a town as Skagway, and famous Arizona lawman, Wyatt Earp, filled in as a volunteer Marshall for 10 days. The town is on the Alaska Marine Highway with a small cruise boat stop, and an exciting trip can be taken on a river boat cruise up the river, viewing wildlife and the Anan Wildlife Observatory and the Wrangell Mountains. Other attractions are the Mount Dewey Overlook, Petroglyph Beach State Park, Chief Shakes Tribal House, Rainbow Falls, and Totem Park.

STIKINE RIVER HUNTS

Grizzlies, black bear and goats

Trout fishing and photo trips in summer

LEE ELLIS

Registered Guide and Outfitter

Box 141 • Wrangell, Alaska

BEAR TOTEM STORES

MRS. WALTER C. WATERS, PROP.

MOST COMPLETE STOCK OF

ALASKA MADE NOVELTIES AND CURIOS

IN THE NORTH

RAW FURS

INDIAN MADE — ESKIMO SLIPPERS

BASKETS — NUGGET & IVORY — CARVED IVORY

MOCCASINS — JEWELRY — BEADS, DOLLS

TOTEM POLES — WATCHES, ETC. — CRIB BOARDS

WRANGELL, ALASKA

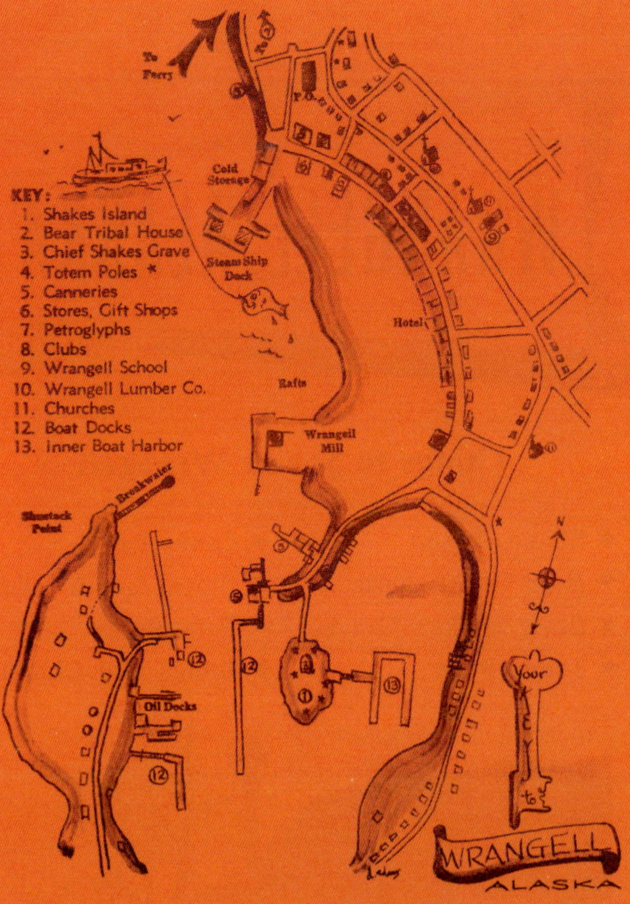

Wrangell, Alaska

This community is the third oldest settlement in Alaska, having been established by the Russians in 1834. It is the only city in Alaska that has been under three flags — Russian, English, and American. The Wrangell Sentinel, a weekly newspaper, printed its first issue November 2, 1902, which makes it the oldest continuous publication in Alaska.

The city is located 800 miles north of Seattle, Washington; and approximately 130 miles southeast of Sitka; 140 miles south of Juneau, the State Capital; and 90 miles north of Ketchikan. Petersburg, a neighboring city of 1,500, is twenty-five miles north and west of Wrangell. Wrangell is the site of old Fort Dionysius, later called Fort Wrangell, which was established by the Russians. It is also the site of the oldest Protestant church in Alaska. A mission was established in 1877. The same year, Alaska's first American school was started and operated four years until destroyed by fire. The school was rebuilt in Sikta.

Excursions

These trips are available to tourists who plan to remain in the area for a day or two:

1. **Grey's Island.** Wonderful fishing, seldom do any boats return without a "King".

2. **Woronkofski.** A boat trip around Woronkofski Island is well worth the effort and cost.

3. **Old Town.** A trip to Old Town, twenty miles to the south, with a stop at Nemo Point, is a must. Fishing is good all the way, and trout can be caught in several streams. Should time permit — continue the trip around Wrangell Island (30 miles long and 5 miles wide), taking in Humpback Bay and Anan Creek, where bears can be seen fishing for salmon. A most interesting two-mile walk can be had on a foot path up Anan Creek, which has a nice look-out cabin. Be sure to take your camera.

4. **Garnet Ledge.** This ledge is about five miles from Wrangell and you can dig yourself a few garnets, and pick wild blackberries in season. Should you be unable to make this trip — you can purchase garnets from the children in Wrangell at a very reasonable price. Wrangell garnets are world known.

Chief Shakes, Wrangell, Alaska

All pictures are actual photographs at Wrangell

HAINES

Haines, Alaska, was named in honor of the first missionary to come to the area, Francina Haines, who arrived in 1879. Haines is connected to the rest of Alaska by the Haines Highway or Haines Cut-off. Its junction with the Alaska Highway at Haines Junction in the Yukon is 152 miles north. It was built by the US Army in 1943 as an alternate route from the Pacific Ocean to the Alaska Highway. Most of the highway follows the old Dalton Trail, used by the Klondike stampeders. Year around access was not achieved until 1963. The town and surrounding native villages are a haven for tourists. One can visit the American Bald Eagle Foundation, Haines Sheldon Museum & Cultural Center, the world's largest collection of hammers from a private collection, the Jilkaat Kwaan Cultural Center in the village of Klukwan, and Fort William N. Seward or Chilkoot Barracks.

This hotel was part of the Sheldon family enterprises, along with many other properties in Haines. The hotel was torn down and the present-day building on Main Street is the office of the Alaska Fjordland Ferry System and sits across the street from the Haines Sheldon Museum. The Fjordland is a high-speed catamaran with service from Haines to Skagway and Juneau. —AC

Utgiagvik, formally Barrow at Point Barrow on the Arctic Ocean is the borough seat of The North Slope Borough, with a population of around 4,000, mostly Inupiat natives. It is an unusual, out of the way, tourist destination with native (Eskimo) culture, the Inupiat Heritage Center, and the Wiley Post-Will Rogers crash site monument. Tours are available with Alaska Airlines from Anchorage and Fairbanks.

Dutch Harbor is a harbor on Amaknak Island in Unalaska in the Aleutian Island chain. It is a major fishing port and is the site of two air attacks by Japanese forces during the 1942 Battle of Midway. It is serviced by the Alaska Marine Highway System and Alaska Airlines. Worth a visit are the Museum of the Aleutians and the Aleutian World War II National Historic Area and related Visitor Center.

Fort William N. Seward was established in 1902 as a US Army post to deal with ongoing border disputes between the US and Canada. During the World War II, it was used as an army recreation center. It was decommissioned in 1947, and a group of war veterans purchased it from the US Government with hopes of creating an arts and commerce community. The fort was 400 acres and had 86 buildings, including a hospital, two barracks buildings, and a fire station. Now the complex has private houses, galleries and shops, an interesting sculpture garden and the historic Hotel Halsingland, which occupies three Jeffersonian-style buildings with a restaurant, bar and library. —AC

SITKA

When people think of Sitka, Alaska, they most often think of history, if they know anything about Alaska. Old town Sitka was founded by Russian-American trader, Alexander Baranof as New Archangel in 1799. Sitka in the Tlinget language means "by the sea." The Sitka National Historic Park/Totem Park was established to commemorate the Battle of Sitka in 1804, the last major conflict between Europeans and native Alaskans. In 1808, the Russians named the area New Archangel and it became the capital of Russian America.

The most outstanding and historic building in the town is St. Michael's Cathedral which was built from 1844–48 and has a great collection of Russian Orthodox art and church artifacts. These two views were taken early in the century. A fire destroyed the church in January 1966, but it was reconstructed to its former glory. Sitka is served by cruise boats and offers a varied number of sites for the tourist; Sitka National Historic Park with both Tlinget and Haida totem poles, the Fortress of the Bear, Alaska Raptor Center, Sitka Sound Science Center, Alaska Native Brotherhood Hall, Russian Bishop's House, Sitka Museum, and the Sheldon Jackson Museum, which opened in 1888 and was purchased by the state in 1885, and Baranof Castle State Historic Site. On Kruzof Island, 15 miles west of Sitka sits the beautiful volcanic dome of Mt. Edgecumbe. Although dormant for hundreds of years, there has been some indication of magma movement.

An early view of Sitka with a cruise boat. —AC

Baranof's Castle on Castle Hill was a two-story log mansion built in 1847 by the Russians. The building burned down in 1894, and the site is now Baranof Castle State Historic Site. This is where the Russians handed over to the United States its new purchase on October 18, 1867. —AC

PRIBILOF ISLANDS

The Pribilof Islands are a group of volcanic islands in the Bering Sea, 200 miles north of Unalaska and 500 northwest of the Siberian coast. St. Paul Island is the main center with a history of birding and seal viewing and has accommodations for visitors. St. George is the other inhabited island with a native population. For years Reeve Aleutian Airways serviced the tourist trade. For Alaska birding trips contact info@birdtrecks.com

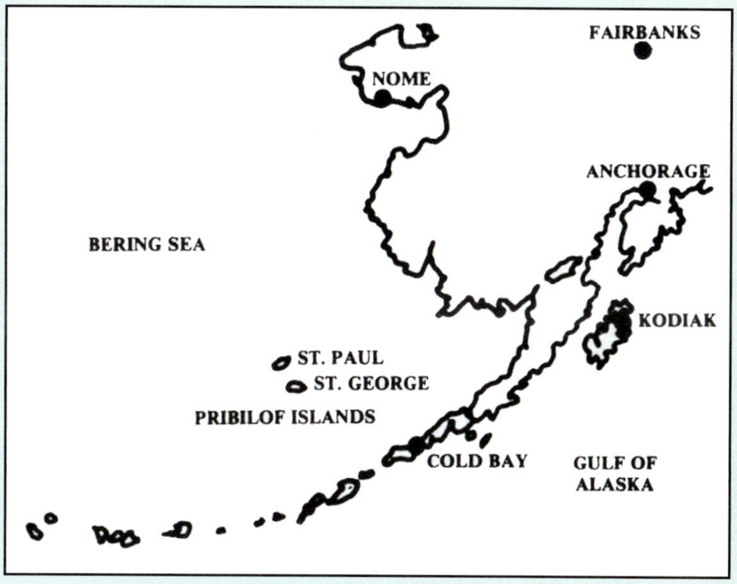

Nome became the next gold rush area starting in 1898, with gold discovered on the beaches by the Bering Sea. By 1900 it was a tent city stretching for 30 miles. As with the Klondike, people came from all over the world to seek their fortunes. The city now is over 50 percent Alaska Native Eskimo. In 1925, there was a diphtheria epidemic and serum was rushed to the site by dog sled. This has now become the famous Iditarod Trail Dog Sled Race. Gold mining and tourism are the main activates, with the new Carrie M. McLain Memorial Museum, the abandoned railroad, many old mining artifacts and diggings outside of town, and a chance to see the Northern Lights at certain times of the year. —AC

An older view of Seward before the March 1964 earthquake and tsunami that forced the town to relocate to higher ground. It is the gateway to the Misty Fiords National Monument. Other attractions include, the port city for the Alaska Railroad, the National Park Visitor Center, Alaska Sealife Center, Seward Community Library and Museum and the famous Mount Marathon Race, held every July 4. —AC

The city of Homer is on Kachemak Bay and has a long land section called the Homer Spit. It has one of the largest populations of bald eagles on the plant. The spit also has beaches, shops, restaurants, and art galleries. The Pratt Museum is in town. —AC

FAIRBANKS

Fairbanks was founded as a gold mining town in 1902 with huge placer deposits worked by dredges for many years. Today it is the northern terminus of the Alaska Railroad and the center of business, finance, and cultural for interior Alaska. There is much to see in town including the University of Alaska's Museum of the North; Morris Thompson Cultural and Visitors Center, Fountainhead Antique Auto Museum; Aurora Ice Museum; the Palace Theater; Gold Dredge 8; the Wickersham House Museum; dog sledding and side trips on the Haul Road and to Arctic Circle Hot Springs and out to North Pole and to the Chena Pump House, and of course all the attractions at Pioneer Park.

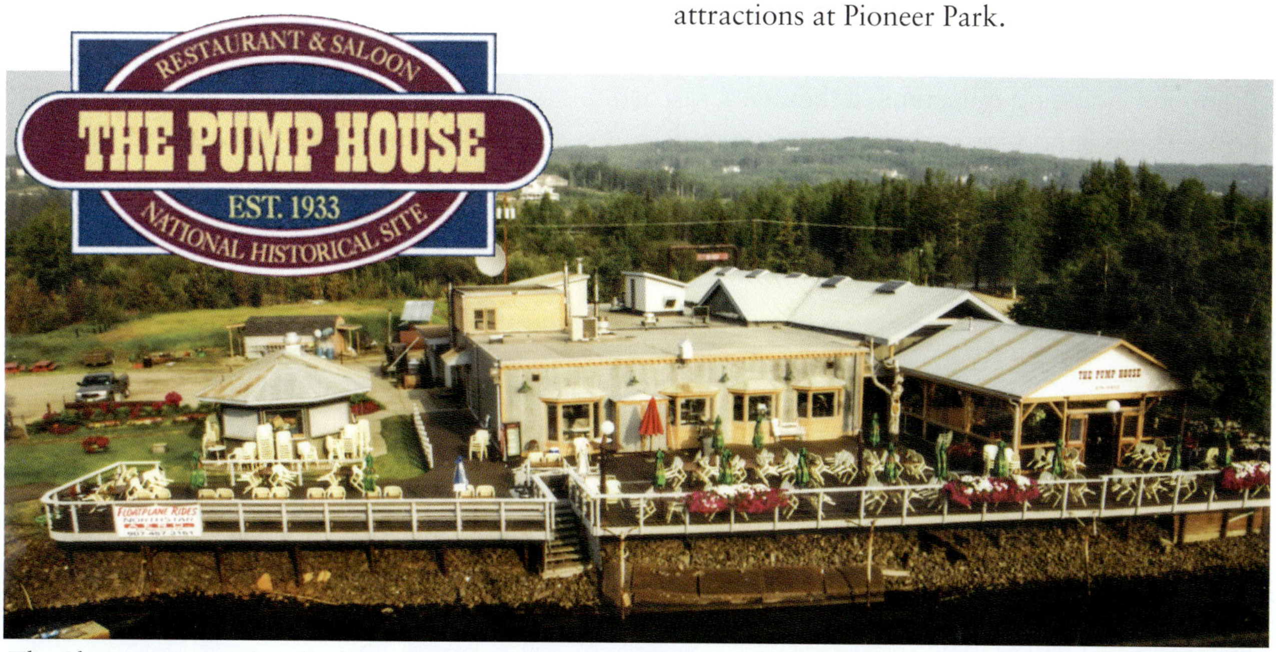

The Chena Pump House also known as the Pump House Restaurant, is located in a shell of a pumping station that was established in 1933 by the Fairbanks Exploration Company to provide water for their dredges operating on Cripple Creek in the Ester area. The company was the largest gold mining operator in Alaska, but the pump house was abandoned in 1958. Twenty years later, it was enlarged and converted into a restaurant with many antiques and original equipment to view. It is listed on the National Register of Historic Places. —ExploreFairbanks.com

One of Fairbanks' best known tourist attractions is the Riverboat Discovery. Jim and Mary Binkley founded the company in 1950 after being asked if they had an interest in operating a local river tour. They had a tour business on the Chena and Tanana rivers using the Godspeed, a converted missionary boat. Jim built Discovery I in his backyard in 1955 and it was put to work right away on the two rivers. It was renovated later to carry more passengers. Discovery II was built on the hull of a freighting steamboat in 1971 and it took over as the main tour boat. Discovery III was built at a shipyard on Whidbey Island in Washington in1987 and took over as the primary boat for tours. After 10 years of being mothballed, Discovery II resumed passenger service and in 2004. Discovery I is was put back in service for special tours and charters. Tour operations are from mid-May until mid-September. At the landing where the boats depart is a dining hall and large gift shop. —Nickolas McGraw

PIONEER PARK

In late 1960 to early 1961, the Pioneers of Alaska requested public land from the state. The plan was to create a tourist attraction that showed historical Alaska exhibits. A non-profit corporation was formed named Pioneer Memorial Park, Inc. In 1965 a request was made to use the 44-acre park for the centennial celebration of the 1867 purchase of Alaska from Russia. The park was opened as "Alaska 67 Centennial Exposition." The next year it was quitclaimed to the State of Alaska and the same day it was given to the City of Fairbanks. It was renamed in the same year "Alaskaland" but in 2002 it reverted back to its original name "Pioneer Park" and became a theme park emphasizing historical Fairbanks as well as serving as a community park. It now has many attractions including museums, a theater, a railroad, a carousel, a pioneer village, restaurants, and shops. There is no fee for entrance to the park, but some of the attractions require one. The park is open from Memorial Day to Labor Day.

Pioneer Park, formerly known as Alaskaland, is in Fairbanks. The S.S. Nenana *boat is in the center, the Pioneer Air Museum in the upper left, and the Harding railroad car in the lower left. The Crooked Creek & Whiskey Island Railroad is on a short loop around the park and the large Civic Center is on the extreme left. The restored town is on the right.*

Part of the restored Gold Rush Town. —All photos on this page from ExploreFairbanks.com

The Nenana *was built in 1933 and had 24 staterooms that held up to 50 passengers. In 1948 it switched from wood to oil for power. It was retired in 1955 and for a short time served as a restaurant and museum on the Chena River. It has had and continues to undergo extensive renovations so that it can reopen in the future. A large model railroad layout with the boat's port of call is inside.*

The railroad car used by President Warren G. Harding when he visited Alaska for the "Golden Spike" ceremony of the Alaska Railroad on July 15, 1923. The car now has a shelter over it.

The Pioneer Air Museum, housed in a large gold-domed building, chronicles the development of flight in Alaska with many original aircraft.

ANCHORAGE

Anchorage, the largest city in Alaska on Cook Inlet, was originally settled as a tent city near the mouth of Ship Creek in 1915, and a planned townsite was platted alongside the bluffs to the south. For the first several decades of its existence, it was primarily used as a port and rail hub by the newly constructed Alaska Railroad. The town grew through the years, especially after World War II, with a population now hovering around 300,000. Today there is much to keep tourists busy and they can visit the Anchorage Alaska Public Lands Information Center in the Old Federal Building, the Alaska Native Heritage Center, the Anchorage Museum at Rasmuson Center, Tony Knowles Coastal Trail, Chugach State Park, Alaska Wildlife Conservation Center, the Alaska Aviation Museum at Lake Hood, along with the seaplane base, the Alaska Zoo, Alaska Railroad Engine #1 at the railroad headquarters, Engine 556 at Delaney Park, Earthquake Park, Kincaid Park and Resolution Park, and many winter sports activities. The Fur Rendezvous winter festival, known as" Fur Rondy" or "Rondy" has been a fixture since 1936. The street view is from the early 1900s.

This 1930s view is of the Anchorage Hotel, the only hotel in the city on the National Register of Historic Places. The original structure was the first wooden building in the "tent city." It was built in 1916 as a two-story "high rise" at the corner of Third Avenue and E Street. In 1936, an annex was constructed across the alleyway on Third Avenue. This 26-room addition is now the main hotel and a skybridge was built connecting the two buildings. For decades this was an elegant place to stay, and many dignitaries stayed here while in town. —AC

KODIAK ISLAND GROUP

The Kodiak Island Group was sighted by the Bering Expedition in 1741, but it was the quest for sea otter pelts that led to Alaska's oldest town. Russian fur traders and hunters swept in and depleted the sea otter herds until Kodiak was reached in 1763 by Stefhen Glotof. Captain James Cook named Kodiak on his trip there in 1778. By 1784, a wealthy Russian merchant and fur trader established the first Russian colony in North America, not far from the present village of Old Harbor. Alexander Baranof arrived in 1791 to take charge of the colony and the next year moved it to the present site of Kodiak. By 1804 the headquarters was transferred to present Sitka. Kodiak is the second largest island in the United States and the largest fishing port in Alaska. In the 1964 earthquake, about 75 percent of the downtown was wiped out but the town has rebounded since. Places to visit include the Kodiak Historical Museum, formally known as the Baranof Museum, the Erskine House, several historic churches and the largest US Coast Guard base in the nation. Fort Abercrombie State Historic Site includes World War II fortifications and a military museum. There is also hunting, sport fishing, and boating.

Bear numbers on the islands are in the thousands, resulting in prime hunting opportunities.

KATMAI NATIONAL PARK AND PRESERVE

Katmai National Park and Preserve is on a peninsula in southern Alaska. It is a wild landscape but is accessible by boat or plane. There are lookout platforms at Brooks Camp that allows people to observe the many brown bears that are drawn there by the salmon runs. The Valley of 10,000 Smokes is an area in the park of lava flows and volcanic ash formed by the massive volcanic eruption that occurred in 1912.

Arne Erickson, a Norwegian, came to Fairbanks in 1909, then to the Iditarod mining district. In 1921, he moved his family to Anchorage. The next year, he was hired to supervise operations of the Crow Creek Mine for its hydraulic placer gold mining. The mine is located just a few miles up the Crow Creek Road from Girdwood, which was destroyed by the 1964 earthquake. He went into a partnership from 1925–33 and continued mining the property until 1938, when it became too expensive to operate. It was one of the largest producing placer gold deposits in Alaska. The family lived on the property and in 1967 it was opened to the public as part of the Alaska Purchase Centennial. Arne died in 1978, the same year the mine was put on the National Register of Historic Places. The Toohey family now owns the property, and it is a major tourist attraction for people to experience a real old gold camp. They are encouraged to dig a shovel-full of dirt from the creek and try their hand at gold panning in large tubs. There is rare mining equipment, beautiful gardens, hiking trails, and amazing mountain scenery. The author spent part of the summer of 1963 on the property as a geologist for the US Forest Service and lived in one of the original miner's cabins.

ALASKA'S SKI AREAS

Alyeska Resort, Eaglecrest Ski Area, Mount Eyak Ski Area, Hill Top Area, Mt. Aurora Skiland, Moose Mountain Ski Resort, Hillberg Ski Area, Birch Hill Area, Ski Lodge, East Peak Resort, Skeetawk Resort, Skiland Ski & Snowboard Area, Hatcher Alpine Experience, Majestic Heli-Ski Resort; Valdez Heli-Ski Guides, Mt. Sima in Whitehorse, the Yukon area

Alyeska Resort at Girdwood, the largest ski resort in the state, has joined the ranks of world-class resorts on the continent. The ski corporation was founded in 1954, and the first chairlift and day lodge were opened in 1959. The roundhouse ski lodge and ski patrol station was built in 1960, and it now houses a museum. There are now 1,400 ski acres serviced by eight lift systems, including an aerial tram. The tram ends three-quarters of the way up the mountain with the terminal, a cafeteria, and the Seven Glaciers 4-star restaurant and bar. At the base of the tram is the modern 300-room Hotel Alyeska. A large housing development surrounds the area. Most of the mountain is geared to the intermediate and advanced skiers but there is also a beginner's area. —AC

It would make sense for a community in Alaska named North Pole to have an establishment such as this. In 1949, the Con Miller family arrived in Alaska and decided to open a clothing store. It closed in 1952, and the family decided to build the first Santa Claus House and general store in a new area, only a short drive from Fairbanks, aptly named North Pole. The general store morphed into the present Santa Claus House as pictured with the largest Santa Claus figure in the world and is now a major tourist attraction. The local post office has been sending letters from Santa to children around the world going on 70 years. —Heather @ Santa Claus House

Near the village of Cantwell on the George Parks Highway is an intriguing four-story, igloo-shaped structure, built of plywood and covered with urethane. It is 80 feet tall and 105 feet wide on a 38-acre plot next to the highway. Years ago, a man named Leo Smith had a dream to build a unique destination hotel. (Smith also built a gas station and a few other small buildings). The building has been abandoned for years and still awaits a buyer to fulfill Smith's dream.

MATANUSKA-SUSITNA VALLEY

The Matanuska-Susitna Valley area in South central Alaska is a tourist paradise. The valley was explored by Russians as far back as 1818. As part of President Roosevelt's New Deal Policy in 1935, 203 families from the United States Midwest region travelled to Alaska and started the Matanuska Valley Colony. The families were chosen due to their cold weather experiences to set up farms in the area. There are sites to explore to keep one busy for a few days or longer. They include the Alpine Historical Park at Sutton, the Museum of Alaska Transportation & Industry at Wasilla, the Musk Ox Farm at Palmer, the Palmer Museum and Visitor Center, the Wasilla Museum & Visitor Center, the restoration of Engine 557 at Wasilla, the Chickaloon Traditional Council, the Knik Museum & Townsite, the Colony House at Palmer, the Iditarod Tral Sled Dog Race headquarters at Wasilla, the Talkeetna Historical Society Museum, the Matanuska Glacier State Recreation Site and the Nancy Lakes State Recreation Area. The Denali State Park offers lots of outdoor options. There is also camping, hiking, and glacier viewing in the state parks and campgrounds.

Hatcher Pass and the Independence Mine State Historic Park

One should not visit the Valley without taking the 49-mile rugged mountain pass road to Hatcher Pass and the remains of the Independence Gold Mining town. Gold miners used the pass in the 1930s and '40s to reach the highly productive gold deposits at the Independence Mine. There is also downhill skiing and hiking in the area of the pass.

NEW COLONISTS FOR MATANUSKA

Officials of the Alaska Rehabilitation Corporation said May 7 more than 30 new applications for land and membership in the Matanuska Valley farming colony had been approved by the United States Department of the Interior.

Officials said these were the first additions to the original 250 families which settled here in 1938 when the colony was first organized.

Bulldozers and other machines will be brought here to assist the newcomers in clearing land and establishing farms.

More than half of the new applications were submitted by war veterans, officials said.

The action indicated a rigid conservationist policy instituted by Secretary Ickes was being relaxed by Secretary of the Interior Krug.

WHITEHORSE, YUKON

Whitehorse, Yukon, was incorporated in 1950, but its history dates to the 1890s Klondike Gold Rush. It lies on the Yukon River and just below the town is Miles Canyon, and formally White Horse Rapid, which was a very dangerous journey for the stampeders to navigate by boat on their long water route to Dawson City. The Whitehorse Dam eventually tamed the river. It was named the capitol of the Yukon Territory on April 1, 1953 and now is the largest city in Northern Canada and the governmental, business, and cultural center of the Yukon. Attractions include the MacBride Museum, the Old Log Church Museum, Yukon Arts Centre, Yukon Beringia Interpretive Centre, Yukon Transportation Museum, Yukon River Tours, and the Yukon Visitor Information Centre. A very popular show for the tourist, Yukon's Frantic Follies vaudeville act, which opened in 1969, finally closed after 48 years in 2017. The city is a major stopping point on the Alaska Highway.

Takhini Hot Springs, (now known as Eclipse Nordic Hot Springs), is one of the most visited locations in the Yukon, in operation for over 100 years and just a 20-minute drive from Whitehorse.

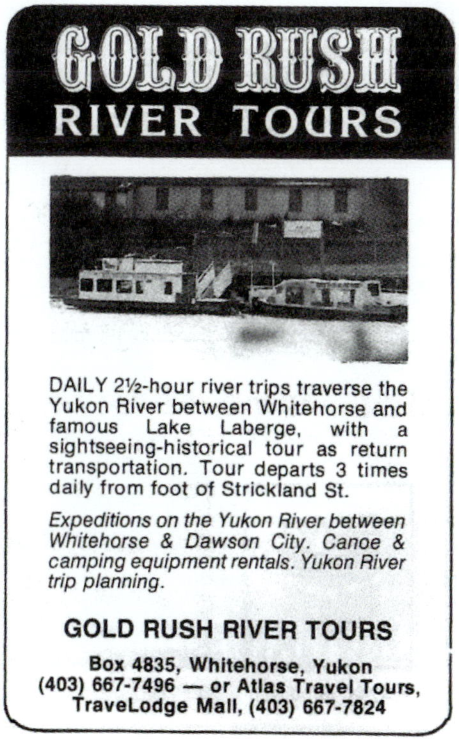

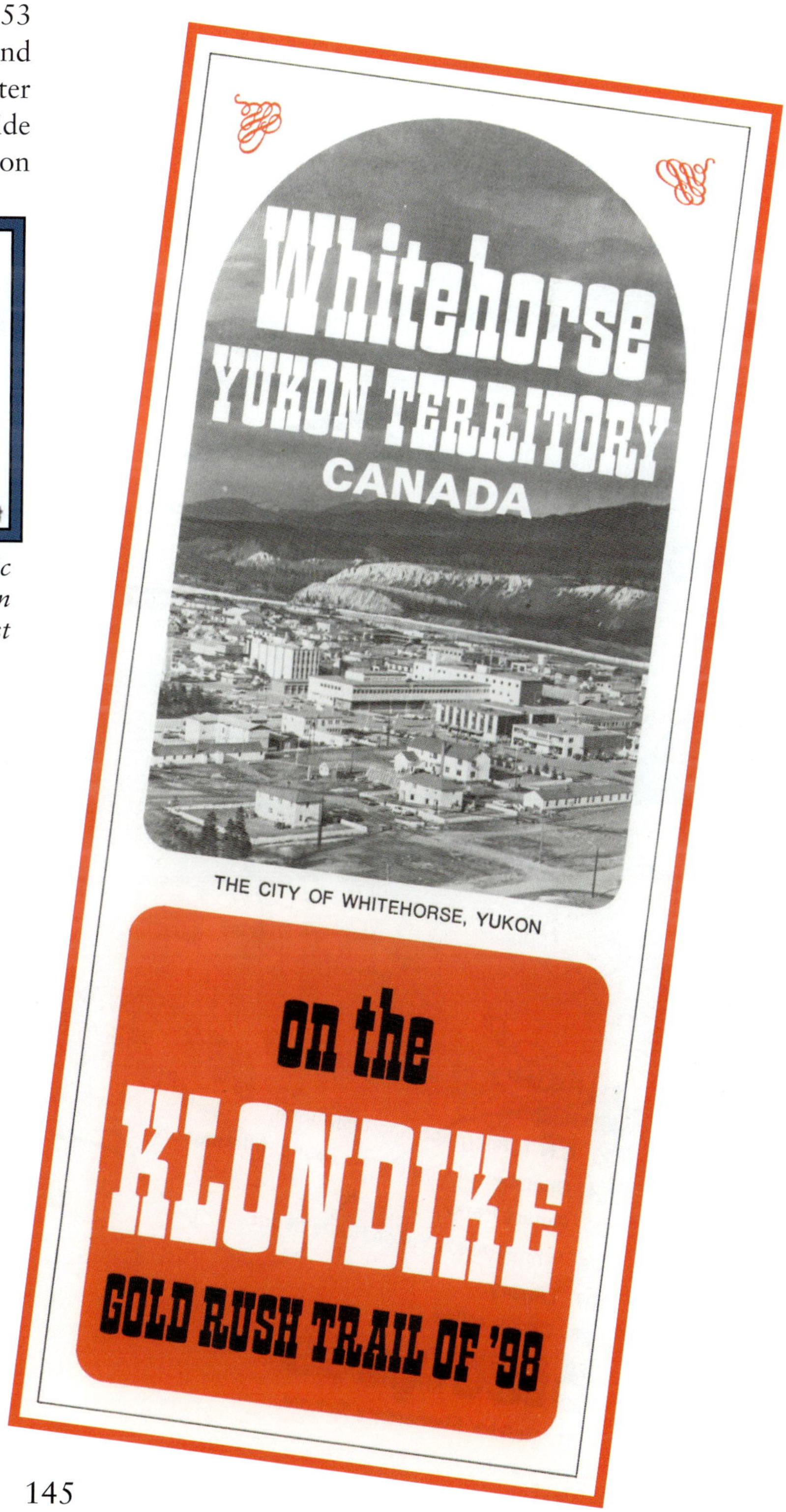

The M.V. Schwatka, *named after a well-known US Army explorer, Frederich Schwatka, traveled up and down Miles Canyon starting in 1960 on a two-hour tour. It operated for over 50 years. In 1922, the 85-foot-long Robert Lowe Suspension Bridge was built across the narrowest and most dramatic part of Miles Canyon cutting through 100-foot basaltic lava rock. Down the channel is the site of old Canyon City, a much-needed stopping point after running the rapids. Several hiking trails are in the area. During the gold rush, a tramway was built along the rapids to skirt the dangerous water.* —AC

Besides the towns of Whitehorse and Dawson City, there is much to see and do in the Yukon. There are five national parks, with Kluane the most accessible, and many other mining towns with museums. Faro, Mayo, and Keno, and other attractions such as the Watson Lake Air Terminal Building, the Northern Lights Space and Science Centre, The Stewart-Cassiar Highway leading south from Watson Lake, the Southern Lake District, The George Johnston Museum at Teslin and the Teslin Tlingit Heritage Center, the Carcross commons with its carving shed and other attractions, the Carcross Desert, the Beaver Creek Visitor Information Centre and the Bordertown Garage and Museum, the St. Elias Mountains and Icefields, the Haines Junction Visitor Information Centre, the Campbell Region Interpretive Centre in Faro, the Faro Arboretum, the Campbell Highway leading to the World War II built CANOL road to the Northwest Territories, the Alpine Interpretive Centre. Old Crow, the only community above the Arctic Circle; the John Tizya Centre, Tombstone Territorial Park and Interpretive Centre, The Dempster Highway, The Klondike Highway and Top of the World Highway, and the ruins of Silver City. Camping, hiking, and water sports are throughout the territory.

COAT OF ARMS of the Yukon Territory
SHIELD: The wavy white and blue vertical stripe represents the Yukon River and refers also to the rivers and creeks where placer gold was discovered and led to the Klondike Gold Rush. The red spire-like forms represent the mountainous country and the gold discs the mineral resources. The St. George's Cross is in reference to the early explorers and fur traders from England who were mainly responsible for the exploration and early development of the Yukon Territory. The roundel in the centre of the cross is a symbol for the fur trade.
CREST: The crest displays a Malamute dog, an animal which has played an important part in the early history of the Yukon, and is noted for its loyalty, stamina and courage.

An older map of the Yukon highways and byways.

DAWSON CITY

Of all the sites in the Yukon, one not to miss is Dawson City. Born of the Great Klondike Gold Rush of the 1890s it is one of the best-preserved mining-era towns in Canada. It can now be reached by plane as well as the Klondike and Top of the World highways and, for the adventurous, by floating the Yukon River hundreds of miles downriver to the city, which lies along the river. It is named after George Mercer Dawson (1849–1901), one of the most eminent geologists of his day. The city is now included in the Klondike Gold Rush International Historical Park with units in the Yukon, British Columbia and Seattle. National Historic Sites in the Dawson City area include the Discovery Claim, *SS Keno*, Dredge No. 4; Robert Service Cabin, Canadian Bank of Commerce, Former Territorial Court House, and the Old Territorial Administration Building. Parks Canada has been instrumental in keeping the gold rush era alive with its many restoration and stabilization efforts.

The Klondike Visitors Association was founded in 1952, with its present name changed in 1960, by a group of Dawson City residents. They dressed up in gold rush attire and began giving tours of the city and gold fields and hosting "Klondike Nights" at the Palace Grand Theater, operating Diamond Tooth Gerties, Jack London's Cabin & Museum, Gold Claim #6, and sponsored other local events.

GuggieVille

Campground - Gold Panning - Showers
Carwash - Hookups - Gift Store - Laundromat
Raw Gold for Sale - Clean & Quiet
3 minutes from Dawson on Bonanza Turnoff
Gordon & Brenda Caley
Box 311, Dawson City YOB 1GO
Phone (403) 993-5008

GuggieVille (now closed) was a very popular campground for years close to the entrance of the Klondike gold fields with views of the massive gold mining activities from 1896 up to World War II. There are present-day mining activities to recover gold that the dredges missed. More recently new ground on the side hills is being mined by hydraulic mining methods.

THE KLONDIKE GOLD RUSH

Gold was discovered in the Klondike River area of the Yukon Territory of Canada in 1896, but it took almost a year for the news to reach the outside world. This would become one of the largest gold strikes in North America and soon a stampede of prospectors headed North by any means possible. People travelled mainly by boat either from the West Coast of the United States or British Columbia, through the Inside Passage of Alaska to the head of the Lynn Canal, then to off load at the newly created towns of Skagway and Dyea. Or by boat on a long journey through the Aleutian Islands of Alaska, to the mouth of the Yukon River, which would carry them up the river to the goldfields and the new town of Dawson City, Yukon. Others would take long trips through the wilderness and largely unexplored areas of Northern Canada and Alaska. Many thought the gold strike was actually in Alaska until they came to the Canadian border. Once everything settled down by 1900, and the White Pass Railway was completed to Whitehorse, tourists started booking trips on the many boats plying the Inside Passage. This opened up the vast territories of both Alaska and the Yukon for development.

An early postcard of Dawson City in its heyday with the huge Moosehide Slide in the far right.

The Old Territorial Administration Building, owned by the Government of Yukon, served the Yukon government until 1953. It now houses the Dawson City Museum with exhibits and artifacts showcasing the city's history through the years. Other historical buildings in Dawson are owned by different entities, including The Yukon Hotel Caley's Store, The Carnegie Library, St. Paul's Church and the Canadian Bankof Commerce. —Michael Gates Photo

2003 Single Day Membership
Diamond Tooth Gerties
Gambling Hall & Can Can Show
Canada's Original Casino
Operated by The Klondike Visitors Assn.
JUL 1 8 2003
$6.00
№ D14696
G.S.T. IS INCLUDED IN PRICE OF MEMBERSHIP
GOOD ONLY ON DATE ISSUED
2003 Single Day Membership

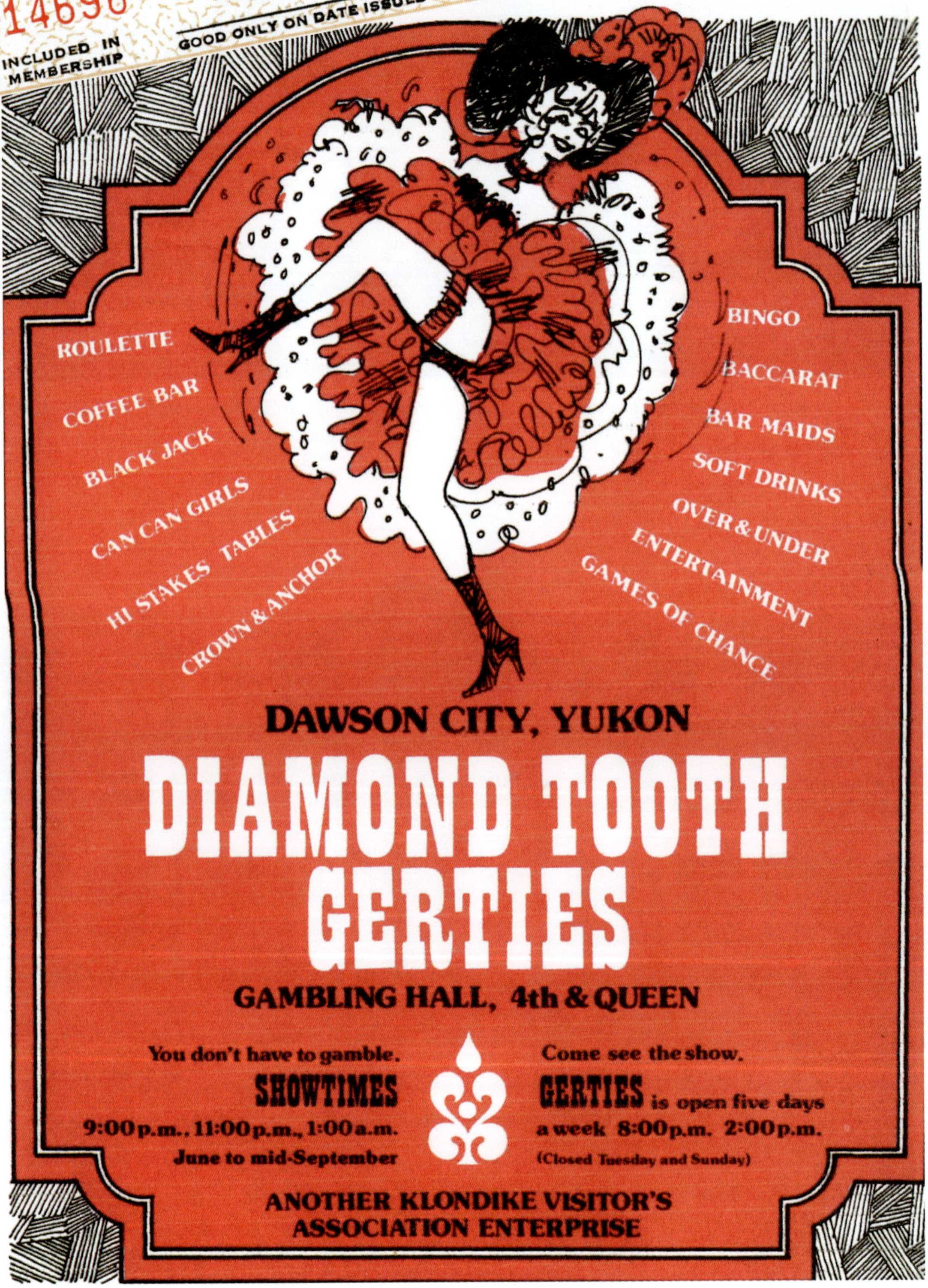
ROULETTE
COFFEE BAR
BLACK JACK
CAN CAN GIRLS
HI STAKES TABLES
CROWN & ANCHOR
BINGO
BACCARAT
BAR MAIDS
SOFT DRINKS
OVER & UNDER
ENTERTAINMENT
GAMES OF CHANCE
DAWSON CITY, YUKON
DIAMOND TOOTH GERTIES
GAMBLING HALL, 4th & QUEEN
You don't have to gamble.
SHOWTIMES
9:00 p.m., 11:00 p.m., 1:00 a.m.
June to mid-September
Come see the show.
GERTIES is open five days a week 8:00 p.m. 2:00 p.m.
(Closed Tuesday and Sunday)
ANOTHER KLONDIKE VISITOR'S ASSOCIATION ENTERPRISE

HISTORIC PALACE GRAND THEATRE

When the Grand Opera House opened in July 1899, it was billed as the biggest and best theatre north of San Francisco and west of Winnipeg. On opening night Dawson turned out in force and although some of the paint was still wet and several stray malamutes had to be ejected, the evening was a great success. For the next few months a wide variety of acts graced its stage and whenever the other entertainment failed, Arizona Charlie would mount the stage in his fringed buckskins and give a demonstration of his marksmanship by shooting glass balls from between his wife's fingers. One night he shot her finger off and she insisted they drop the act.

In October, 1899, "The Grand" became "The Palace Grand". A year later it was renamed the "Savoy". During this period various owners changed the layout, the lobby lost the bar and gained a shooting gallery. The theatre finally became "The Auditorium" and saw everything from legitimate theatre to bazaars and dances. Finally called the Klondike Nugget Dance Hall in the '30's, the old building continued to entertain thousands until 1940 when it was closed.

Reconstruction of the theatre was attempted in 1960, but was not possible due to the effects of permafrost. After careful study of ***each and every detail***, the structure was dismantled piece by piece and a complete replica of the original 1899 building was reconstructed. In 1962, the new Palace Grand Theatre was officially opened.

Today the theatre is owned by Parks Canada and each summer is leased to the Klondike Visitors Association for the locally produced Gaslight Follies!

The KVA stopped leasing the theater in 2003. It has been closed for entertainment since that time, but Parks Canada does rent it out occasionally. The show brought to life for tourists a glimpse into the life and times during the famous gold rush.

The showplace of Dawson, possibly at the time of its opening in July 1899. —AC

For many years this theater provided entertainment for the tourist visiting Dawson City. —Michael Gates Photo

—AC

The commissioner's residence was built in 1901 to provide a permanent home. The house had electricity, hot air heat and an elegant gingerbread appearance outside. Inside plumbing was added in 1903. After a disastrous fire in 1906, it was rebuilt in 1908 to its present appearance today. A second-story sun-room was added in 1914, but in 1916 the building was closed and ceased to operate as the official residence. In 1950, the building was acquired by the Sisters of Ann and operated as home for the aged until 1963 when it was again closed. In 1973, Parks Canada took over the building and substantial renovation work has been done. —Michael Gates Photo

SOME WONDERS OF DAWSON

In Land of 24 Hours Endless Daylight

IN DAWSON

1. Magnificent Panorama from the Midnight Dome, overlooking city.
2. Cottage Home of Robert W. Service, famous Bard of Yukon.
3. Picturesque old Dance Halls and Romantic Resorts.
4. Moosehide Indian Village, home of the original Montezumas of Klondike.
5. Virgin Gold Dust, Nuggets, Rare Furs, Mastodon Ivory, Nugget Jewelry, Indian Baskets and Beaded Moose Skin Handiwork.
6. Beautiful sub-Arctic Flowers growing in profusion—Also Gardens and Fields.
7. Famous Tourist Midnight-Daylight Dance in Arctic Brotherhood Hall, when tourist boats are in port.
8. The famous "Slide" on the mountain back of Dawson; theme of strange Indian legends.
9. The flag on crest of "Midnight Dome," back of Dawson. Watch for it from the boat.
10. Picturesque dog teams of famous native Huskies and Malamutes.
11. Shrine to six hundred Yukoners who served in Great War.

DAWSON'S GREAT GOLD CREEKS

1. Largest Gold Dredges in the World.
2. Greatest Hydraulic Gold Works.
3. Picturesque Klondike River—Best fishing in world for grayling or Arctic trout.
4. Wonderful individual gold mines.
5. Hunker Summit and King Solomon Dome, viewing source of all the great gold creeks and 200 miles of snowy crest of the Rocky Mountains.
6. Historic scenes of world's most romantic and greatest gold strike and stampede.
7. Glorious midnight sun and cloud effects.
8. Hundreds of miles of "tailings" from the greatest gold mining operations in the world.
9. Demonstrations of gold mining and washing.
10. Wonderful "White Channel" which carries the great pay-streak of gold.
11. Bear Creek Village, shops and mining scenes, and giant siphon.
12. Picturesque and hospitable roadhouses.
13. Silver Gray Fox Farms.

Dawson is only 40 hours' ride from Skagway by luxurious trains and steamers, and the outfitting center for moose, caribou, bear and mountain sheep hunters.

—Circa early 1920s

DREDGES

Dredges were brought into the Klondike Valley in 1899 as a very efficient, but very destructive, means of getting every ounce of gold out of the ground. Dredge #4 is the largest wooden-hull dredge in North America and has become a major tourist attraction for visitors to the gold fields. It was built on Bonanza Creek in 1912 and operated until 1959, leaving huge tailing piles as it created its own pond ahead and left the tailings behind it. Its onboard sluice boxes could gather even the finest bit of gold that was never mined by hand. The Yukon Ditch completed in 1909, brought in water from long distances. This water was essential for the mining process and was used to supply the necessary electricity to operate the dredges. Yukon Consolidated Gold Company, or YCGC, controlled most of the dredging operations until the end. When #4 was shut down it remained in place and slowly sank into the muck. In 1991–92, Parks Canada began extensive restoration on the dredge, freeing it from 18 feet of icy silt and mud. It was done with help from the Canadian military, which had experience with large projects such as this. It was excavated, refloated, and eventually relocated on land at its current location. The sinking preserved all the inner workings of the dredge, including the tools to keep the mammoth dredge in operation. In the spring of 1993, access bridges were built to the main deck for viewing and the dredge was opened to the public on July 10, 1993. Work is continuing on the restoration efforts. It is now a National Historic Site, located about six miles up the Bonanza Creek Road.

—PARKS CANADA